TIME FOR A
Heart 2 Heart
WITH GOD

An Interactive Study Guide
for Change of Heart: Never Say Never Novel

NIKKI R. MILLER

TIME FOR A Heart 2 Heart WITH GOD
An Interactive Study Guide for Change of Heart: Never Say Never Novel

Published by Change of Heart Movie, LLC. Copyright © 2020 by Change of Heart Movie, LLC. All rights reserved.

Ordering Information:
Books may be purchased by contacting the publisher, Change of Heart Movie, LLC by email at changeofheartmovie@gmail.com.

Cover design: Enigma Graphics
Formatting: Chris Betchley

ISBN: 978-0-9977592-2-8 (Paperback)
ISBN: 978-0-9977592-3-5 (eBook)

Unless otherwise noted, Scripture quotations are taken from the King James version.
Printed in the United States of America

Table of Contents

Foreword

Nikki R. Miller is the author of the amazing novel, "Change of Heart: Never Say Never". It is a wonderful story of redemption that shows the way to recover from any hurt or tragedy through the power of forgiveness. Everyone will be able to find in its pages not only a compelling story, but help and healing for their own lives.

This latest release, Time For A Heart 2 Heart With God, is an insightful step by step study guide to assist you in getting the most out of "Change of Heart". It is designed to be used by an individual as well as group study. In its pages the Holy Spirit will challenge you and bring spiritual growth. You will not be the same person by the end of this study.

Nikki and her husband, Dr. Johnny Miller, have been active and faithful members of our church for over 5 years. They live out the call of God on their lives every day. It is Nikki's purpose in the novel and the study guide to share with others the same freedom that she has received in Christ.

May you be blessed as you take this journey.

~Pastor Linda Hufton~
World Harvest Church, Roswell, GA

Introduction

There are many people walking around with locked hearts. Hearts that have been broken and wounded for one reason or another. Whether you realize it or not, the key to unlocking your broken and wounded heart is forgiveness. Forgiveness of a tremendous hurt can only be accomplished with the help of God. And the only way to do that is by surrendering your WHOLE heart to Him. Have you suffered a tremendous hurt and cannot seem to let it go? If your answer is yes, then it's time for a heart 2 heart with God.

Forgiveness is the common denominator for every hurt. It is the "key" to your freedom and peace for which God is waiting to unlock for you if you allow Him to do so. There are a lot of lessons that can be taken from this story. Each chapter of the "Change of Heart: Never Say Never" novel has some kind of takeaway that you can apply to your own life. And I am sure each of you can relate to at least one of the characters in this story. Everyone has been hurt at some point in their lives. The question is…

How do you handle or how have you handled the hurt you have experienced? Some may see that they have handled their hurt just fine, and some may see that they have tried; however, just cannot let it go. Now is the time to do so and do it in the right way.

This interactive study guide will help you do a self-check to see if your heart is in the right place and at the same time, have a little fun while you're at it! You will see for yourselves what I am talking about as you begin exploring the different chapters of this study guide. **Please be aware that all excerpts from the novel will not be in the exact order how it's read; however, will indicate the page numbers for you to easily find them.** This interactive study guide can be worked individually or as a group.

Are you ready? Time for YOUR Heart 2 Heart with God!

~Nikki R. Miller~

Chapter 1

"Got Mercy?"

"Yeah, I know. He'll see where I was, on Sunday after he get his gift,' she said. 'God always bless us with things we don't deserve. That is what you call mercy, Junior… Something we get over and over again, even when we do wrong.' Rose shared with her son, instilling that truth in him." (pg. 6)

Rose is right! God is a merciful God, and He extends His mercy to us every single day. Mercy and forgiveness actually go hand and hand. He continues to bless us even when we don't deserve it sometimes. Can you imagine what the world would be like if God held a grudge against us every time we sinned? Think about it for a moment…

I'm so glad He tells us in His word…

Proverbs 10:22

"The blessing of the LORD, it maketh rich, and he addeth no sorrow with it."

Micah 7:18

"Who is a God like unto thee, that pardoneth iniquity, and passeth by the transgression of the remnant of his heritage? he retaineth not his anger for ever, because he delighteth in mercy."

Titus 3:5

"Not by works of righteousness which we have done, but according to his mercy he saved us, by the washing of regeneration, and renewing of the Holy Ghost;"

Food for thought:

Plain and simple, remember to extend mercy to others as God extends mercy to you over and over again.

Here are some questions for you to consider:

1. Do you feel you deserve everything you get whether it is good or bad?

2. Name 2 important gifts you have received that you feel you did not deserve.

3. Do *you* extend mercy often? *(Yes or No)*

4. Describe briefly where you extended mercy to someone and you felt they did not deserve it.

5. How do you feel now, IF you answered #4 with someone?

Chapter 2

"Façade Or Factual"

"They were dressed in their Sunday best: Calvin Sr. with a black polyester suit, white dress shirt and a matching paisley tie and handkerchief that was white, purple and black. Every strand of hair was laying down on his head to show he had a fresh haircut and not one hair was sticking out of his mustache or goatee." (pg. 7)

We see Calvin Sr. dressed to a tee and ready for his Deacon duties, however, the inner man operates on a totally different agenda. Some people would rather put up a front on the outside than deal with the root of a problem or hurt going on inside. After reading Chapter 1, we can clearly see that Calvin Sr. is living a lie.

Let's see what God has to say about facades…

Matthew 23:28

"Even so ye also outwardly appear righteous unto men, but within ye are full of hypocrisy and iniquity."

1 Samuel 16:7

"But the LORD said unto Samuel, Look not on his countenance, or on the height of his stature; because I have refused him: for the LORD seeth not as man seeth; for man looketh on the outward appearance, but the LORD looketh on the heart."

1 Peter 3:3-4

"Whose adorning let it not be that outward adorning of plaiting the hair, and of wearing of gold, or of putting on of apparel; But let it be the hidden man of the heart, in that which is not corruptible, even the ornament of a meek and quiet spirit, which is in the sight of God of great price."

Food for thought:

Do you think Calvin Sr.'s behavior at home and at church is driven by past hurt? It's certainly possible. It can simply be just insecurity. Did you know that even something as simple as "insecurity" can be caused by hurt or trauma? It is not something that just develops out of nowhere. And whether it's insecurity or something else, the devil uses that hurt (whatever it is) to cause you to sin in some way. That is why it is important to address hurt as soon as possible… for peace of mind, healing of the heart and pure freedom!

Here are some questions for you to consider:

1. Have you ever worn a façade or put up a front for anyone, like maybe family, friends, co-workers, your church family? *(Now be honest with yourself. That is the first step to being free of any past hurt.)*

2. If you are currently putting up a front or façade, what is causing you to do so? If you did this in the past, what caused you to do it? *(Again, be honest with yourself)*

3. What do you think people gain from wearing a façade or putting up a front?

Chapter 3

"Don't Let 'It' Pull Your Trigger"

"With less excitement, Calvin Jr. said, 'Happy Birthday, Daddy,' as he remembered how he treated his mom when she returned home from buying that watch." (pg. 16)

Calvin Jr.'s anger from a few nights before his dad's birthday dinner began to kindle as he remembered the way his dad blew up at his mom. Sometimes certain events, dates, places, people, or things can trigger bad memories, igniting the hurt or pain you've experienced. It's the mind where all of those memories are kept stored. How do you quiet the mind during these times and not let those memories pull your trigger?

The word of God says in…

Psalm 37:8

"Cease from anger, and forsake wrath: fret not thyself in any wise to do evil."

Ephesians 4:26-27

"Be ye angry, and sin not: let not the sun go down upon your wrath: Neither give place to the devil."

Romans 12:17-21

"Recompense to no man evil for evil. Provide things honest in the sight of all men. If it be possible, as much as lieth in you, live peaceably with all men. Dearly beloved, avenge not yourselves, but rather give place unto wrath: for it is written, Vengeance is mine; I will repay, saith the Lord. Therefore if thine enemy hunger, feed him; if he thirst, give him drink: for in so doing thou shalt heap coals of fire on his head. Be not overcome of evil, but overcome evil with good."

Food for thought:

Now, I know that last one is a hard pill to swallow; however, we must put forth every effort to do what it says. If we keep our mind busy with these verses (and there are more), it will be hard to pull your trigger.

Here are some questions for you to consider:

1. Name 1-3 things you do to control your temper when you become angry.

2. Have you ever sought revenge on someone that did you wrong? *(Yes or No)* Be honest…

3. If so, did you regret doing so afterwards? *(Yes or No)*

If not, maybe you do now after this study…

Chapter 4

"Don't Pass On Your Passion"

"He lost the love of playing football after his dad left, and really wasn't interested in other sports and activities." (pg. 31)

"He majored in Engineering while T.B. majored in Communications. Calvin's goal was to become a project manager for commercial construction projects, although deep inside, his passion had always been to be a professional football player." (pg. 32)

I believe God is the one who plants our passion(s) and gift(s) inside of us, which are to be used in bringing glory to His name. Here we see Calvin Jr. has allowed his dad's mistakes to draw him away from his passion of playing football. Now, is he happy with pursuing Engineering? Maybe, but he will never know what blessings God had in store for him for that specific passion since he did not pursue playing football.

The word of God says in…

Proverbs 16:9

"A man's heart deviseth his way: but the LORD directeth his steps."

Proverbs 19:21

"There are many devices in a man's heart; nevertheless the counsel of the LORD, that shall stand."

Jeremiah 29:11

"For I know the thoughts that I think toward you, saith the LORD, thoughts of peace, and not of evil, to give you an expected end."

1 John 2:27

"But the anointing which ye have received of him abideth in you, and ye need not that any man teach you: but as the same anointing teacheth you of all things, and is truth, and is no lie, and even as it hath taught you, ye shall abide in him."

Food for thought:

Never allow anything or anyone to cause you to pass on your passion(s). If you do, you may regret passing later on in life. Your passion(s) is part of your purpose in life. It is what brings you joy and happiness, when you are actively doing what God put in your heart to do. And again, it GLORIFIES Him.

Here are some questions for you to consider:

1. Name 1-3 passion(s) you have that you know came directly from God. *Memory Jogger: It could be something you used to do as a little child.*

2. Are you now actively pursuing your passion(s)? *(Yes or No)*

3. If not, what is keeping you from doing so?

Whatever it is, God has exactly what you need to do whatever He has placed in your heart to do!

Chapter 5

"Don't Rain On My Parade"

"Among the few who were mustering up the courage to stand and go up there was Corey; however, Calvin intercepted by grabbing his arm and asked, 'Where are you going?'

'Up there,' he told his dad as he pondered why his father was stopping him. Calvin then asked, 'Why?' Elaina, Katrina and David were all puzzled by Calvin's actions. When he realized what he was doing, he let go of his son's arm. 'I feel I need to, Dad,' Corey said and continued to the altar." (pg. 41)

Wow, somebody is raining on Corey's parade, or better yet, trying to keep him from receiving his tailored made blessing from God. This was the most important thing that Corey could have ever done in his life, and his own dad doesn't want it. This kind of behavior, my friend, is driven by none other than Satan himself. Remember, hurting people hurt people and most of the time, it happens right in your *own* family.

The word of God says in…

Philippians 2:3

"Let nothing be done through strife or vainglory; but in lowliness of mind let each esteem other better than themselves."

James 3:16

"For where envying and strife is, there is confusion and every evil work."

1 Peter 5:8

"Be sober, be vigilant; because your adversary the devil, as a roaring lion, walketh about, seeking whom he may devour:"

Food for thought:

You should never stop or discourage anyone from advancing in life just because you are not advancing. Instead, you should encourage them and cheer them on, especially when the advancing leads to developing their relationship with God.

Here are some questions for you to consider:

1. Have you ever been jealous or envious of someone because they progressed in an area of life more so than you? *(Yes or No)* Be honest…

2. If you answered yes, do you still envy them? Or did you finally cheer them on, encourage, and/or pray for them? Be honest…

3. Let's flip the switch… Has anyone ever rained on your parade? *(Yes or No)*

4. If so, how did you react?

If you're comfortable, discuss your reaction with your group *(if you're doing the study guide as a group)*, **and see how others would've reacted to your situation.**

Chapter 6

"To Forgive, Or Not To Forgive, That Is The Question"

"Calvin said, 'Laina, I'll never forgive my dad for what he did. He don't deserve it!'

'Well, when did you become God? Do you know He could say the same thing about you, but He doesn't? You're only hurting yourself by carrying around all this anger and bitterness against him.'" *(pg. 51-52)*

Elaina is right. Who gave Calvin the permission of not allowing his dad to be forgiven? Certainly not God, because in His word, it says different. Calvin is so angry with his dad that forgiving him is not even an option for him, even though his mom had forgiven his dad. It is because he really looked up to his dad and thought the world of him.

To forgive, or not to forgive, that is the question… Well God has the answer!

Colossians 3:13

"Forbearing one another, and forgiving one another, if any man have a quarrel against any: even as Christ forgave you, so also do ye."

Luke 6:37

"Judge not, and ye shall not be judged: condemn not, and ye shall not be condemned: forgive, and ye shall be forgiven."

Luke 17:3-4

"Take heed to yourselves: If thy brother trespass against thee, rebuke him; and if he repent, forgive him. And if he trespass against thee seven times in a day, and seven times in a day turn again to thee, saying, I repent; thou shalt forgive him."

Food for thought:

Obviously, God is serious about this forgiving thing. That means EVERYONE deserves to be forgiven, even yourself. And He states over and over again, if you don't forgive, He won't forgive you of your sins.

Here are some questions for you to consider:

1. Have you ever felt someone did you wrong and did not deserve to be forgiven *(including yourself [i.e. if you are a female, you had an abortion and have never forgiven yourself for doing so, or if you are a male, you allowed or pushed someone to have an abortion])? (Yes or No)* Be honest…

2. If so, please explain briefly why you felt this person should not be forgiven?

3. Take a moment and think about those who may have hurt you in some kind of way, past or present. Now write their names down. *(For your eyes only)*

4. If you have written down any name(s), have you forgiven them? *(Yes or No)*

If not, here is your *first* opportunity to do so.

Chapter 7

"Nobody Is Perfect, Not Even You"

"Calvin replied with a slight smile, 'And I guess you live without sin now.'

'I didn't say that. Nobody's perfect, C.J. That's why we need God… to put us in check sometimes. You know how that is.'" (pg. 55)

T.B. hit it right on the nose when he said, 'Nobody's perfect, C.J. That's why we need God… to put us in check sometimes.' God, our Heavenly Father, is the only perfect one. Unfortunately, not us, no matter how hard we try. There are so many people who want to be perfect, think they are perfect, or think that they have arrived; however, that just won't happen, at least not on our own.

The word of God says in…

Romans 3:23-24

"For all have sinned, and come short of the glory of God; Being justified freely by his grace through the redemption that is in Christ Jesus."

Ecclesiastes 7:20

"For there is not a just man upon earth, that doeth good, and sinneth not."

1 John 1:8-10

"If we say that we have no sin, we deceive ourselves, and the truth is not in us. If we confess our sins, he is faithful and just to forgive us our sins, and to cleanse us from all unrighteousness. If we say that we have not sinned, we make him a liar, and his word is not in us."

Food for thought:

Bottom line… we are only made perfect and righteous through Jesus Christ, the son of God; therefore, if you want to try and have that perfect life *(happy and without sin)*, then you need to make sure He lives on the inside of you along with another gift of God, the Holy Spirit. Did someone say, "Who is the Holy Spirit?" I'm so glad you asked! He is our comforter, helper, the one who sets us free, and teaches us ALL things in Jesus' name. He also inspires us to remember every word Jesus told us (John 14:26).

Here are some questions for you to consider:

1. In 2 Corinthians 5:21 it says, "For he hath made him to be sin for us, who knew no sin; that we might be made the righteousness of God in him."   What does this mean to you?

2. What steps have you taken or are taking to ensure you are living the *most* perfect life that you can?

3. A *perfect* life looks different for everyone. What does *that* perfect life look like for you?

**And then just for a fun break, say "life, look, like" really fast, speeding up each time. How many times can you say it without fumbling over the words?

Chapter 8

"Lend A Hand When You Can"

"'So, why don't you help him, Dad?' suggested Corey. 'Since you didn't get a chance to play like you wanted to, you can live vicariously through David,' Corey explained with a smile. Elaina came over from washing dishes and laid her hand on Corey's shoulder and told him, 'That's an excellent idea, Corey.' She stood there for a moment to see what Calvin's response was going to be. As a matter of fact, all eyes were on him. Calvin replied, 'I'll think about it.'" (pg. 64)

"'Daddy, can you start helping me next Saturday with football?' David asked. He figured if he asked his dad again, he would go ahead and just say yes." (pg. 66)

There really should not be any second thoughts when it comes to helping someone become better in their craft or calling, especially if you have the experience to do so. Calvin should not have had to think twice about helping his own son better his football skills since that's an area of expertise for him. Sounds like he's allowing what happened in the past to get in the way of being a blessing to his own son and can potentially hold his son back from becoming all God has called him to be. As parents, we should desire the best for our children. And to be honest, whether we are parents or not, we as children of God should desire the best for one another as God wants His best for us… His children.

The word of God says in…

Hebrews 13:6

"So that we may boldly say, The Lord is my helper, and I will not fear what man shall do unto me."

Proverbs 11:27

"He that diligently seeketh good procureth favour: but he that seeketh mischief, it shall come unto him."

Philippians 2:4

"Look not every man on his own things, but every man also on the things of others."

Food for thought:

As you help and bless others, God will do the same for you. God blesses us with gifts and talents to share with the world, therefore bringing glory to His name. So, don't be stubborn. Use your gift(s) and talent(s) to bless others. You never know how it will impact someone in need of what you have.

Here are some questions for you to consider:

1. What do you feel your gift(s) and/or talent(s) are?

2. How are you using your gift(s) and/or talent(s) to help others?

3. Was there ever a time in your life where you knew your gift(s) and/or talent(s) could have helped some-one in need; however, for some reason, you did not offer your help? *(Yes or No)* Be honest… If yes, what was the reason for not helping them?

4. And if you had the opportunity again to offer your help to them, would you? *(Yes or No)* Briefly explain your answer either way.

Chapter 9

"Who Are You Really?"

"'I've got to do something with this hair,' Patrice said to herself as she looked in the mirror in the bathroom while at her corporate apartment in Southfield. She picked through her frizzy hair and said to herself, 'I hope it wasn't like this in front of Tony.' Her hair was hanging down with fallen curls. She had changed out of the clothes she had on into something more relaxing. She took the hair scrunchy that was sitting on the sink by her cell phone and pulled her hair up in it." (pg. 68)

When we first meet someone, we typically want to make a good impression. It doesn't matter if it's a first date, or you could be a student desiring to make a good impression on your teacher so they can see you're a good student. Whatever the reason, you never *really* know a person just by *looking* at them.

So, let's take a break here and have a little fun with a game called "Two Truths And A Tale!"

How to play "Two Truths And A Tale"

For this great get-to-know-you game, each person must make three statements about themselves, where one of which is not true.

For example: I have two brothers, I was born in Australia, I have a motorcycle.

This works best when you give the group some time to think of their statements and write them down if they need to.

Once one person makes their statements, the rest of the group must guess or vote on which statement is the tale. It could work well to get each group member to write down their own answers and see who gets the most correct.

Have fun!

Chapter 10

"Me Time"

In this chapter, there will not be an excerpt from the novel. The focus will be simply to just make sure you do self-care. It doesn't matter if you are a female or male, pampering yourself sometimes is essential. It reduces stress, can keep you healthy, and helps you to stay grounded. So, a little **"me time"** is quite alright. That's what Patrice did in order to get a fresh look and a fresh start with T.B. Sometimes we just need a *fresh* start or pick-me-up.

The word of God even talks about taking care of yourself. What this means is, **you must love yourself** and not treat your body just any way. That includes your heart.

Here's what it says…

1 Corinthians 6:19-20

"What? know ye not that your body is the temple of the Holy Ghost which is in you, which ye have of God, and ye are not your own? For ye are bought with a price: therefore glorify God in your body, and in your spirit, which are God's."

Mark 6:31

"And he said unto them, Come ye yourselves apart into a desert place, and rest a while: for there were many coming and going, and they had no leisure so much as to eat."

Ephesians 5:29-30

"For no man ever yet hated his own flesh; but nourisheth and cherisheth it, even as the Lord the church: For we are members of his body, of his flesh, and of his bones."

Food for thought:

Self-care is none other than showing love to YOU! Your mind, body, and soul make up YOU! So, make sure you are showing love to all three by not allowing ANY negative intentions to take root in your mind, body *(this includes the mouth)*, or your soul *(your heart)*.

Here are some questions for you to consider:

1. What are 2-3 things you do for self-care?

2. Now, if you are comfortable, share to the group what you do for self-care. *(You may have a new self-care idea for others to try.)*

Take care of YOU!

Chapter 11

"Keep Your Eyes On The Prize"

"Patrice eyed Calvin quickly from head to toe. He was dressed in some nice dark blue jeans with a sky blue, long sleeved collar shirt and a dark brown leather belt that matched his loafers. His wife was dressed just as fashionable as she had on a cute long sleeve fall top, dark blue jeans, and dark brown boots that came up just below the knee. However, her attire didn't seem to get Patrice's attention as much as Calvin's did. Elaina took notice of the attention that Patrice gave her husband, and she began mulling over how Calvin knew this Patrice woman." (pg. 77)

Patrice clearly has her mind and eyes set on something she is not supposed to. We must remember to keep our eyes on the prize, the right prize that is, and that prize is the kingdom of God… certainly not someone else's husband or wife. Satan will use any and every distraction possible to get you off course and away from God. In this case, he's testing Elaina, who's been saved for a while; however, she handled the situation perfectly. Who knows, she probably could have silently asked God what to do in that moment, which in my opinion is the best way to make sure we keep our eyes on the prize.

Here are some tips from the word of God on how to keep your eyes on the prize especially during times of testing…

James 4:7

"Submit yourselves therefore to God. Resist the devil, and he will flee from you."

1 Corinthians 9:24-25

"Know ye not that they which run in a race run all, but one receiveth the prize? So run, that ye may obtain. And every man that striveth for the mastery is temperate in all things. Now they do it to obtain a corruptible crown; but we an incorruptible."

Hebrews 12:1-2

"Wherefore seeing we also are compassed about with so great a cloud of witnesses, let us lay aside every weight, and the sin which doth so easily beset us, and let us run with patience the race that is set before us, Looking unto Jesus the author and finisher of our faith; who for the joy that was set before him endured the cross, despising the shame, and is set down at the right hand of the throne of God."

<u>Food for thought:</u>

The more time you spend with God, the easier it becomes to fight back when being tested by Satan. By ourselves, we are no match for him; however, with God, we are more than conquerors *(See Romans 8:37)* and will be able to endure the race set before us!

Here are some questions for you to consider:

1. Was there ever a time where you could see clearly you were being tested by Satan and had to make a quick decision on how to handle the situation before it got out of hand? *(Yes or No)* If there were multiple situations, pick the one that had the greatest impact on you.

2. How did you handle it?

3. Looking back, could you have handled the situation in a better way? *(Yes or No)*

4. If yes, what would you have done differently to make sure your eyes were kept on the prize?

Chapter 12

"Leave Well Enough Alone"

"'Patrice... what are you still doing here?' Calvin asked, when he noticed her walking in the hallway past the glass window of his office at Kenner & Welles Inc. He ceased from reviewing some documents and quickly got up, peeking out of his office to get her attention." (pg. 80)

"'I'm headed to the cafeteria. You want me to get you something?' she asked him. 'It's the least I can do for ruining you and Tony's male bonding time.'

Calvin took a quick glance at his watch to see what time it was and said, 'Well, I haven't had anything to eat yet for lunch. Why don't I join you, if you're okay with that? Then you won't have to eat by yourself.'" (pg. 81)

There was no harm done by Calvin in speaking to Patrice when she passed by his office; however, he should have just left well enough alone. He just *had* to ask to join her for lunch. Some of you are probably asking what is the harm in joining her for lunch? In an actual situation like this, there may not be a problem with it; however, it can open the door for Satan to test you *(married man or woman)*, therefore, making it into a problem later on down the line. In Calvin's situation, this becomes a playground for Satan because of what Calvin Sr. did. And why not lead his son down the same path... if not in church, then at work? Can you say hook, line, and sinker.

Here's what Satan is all about for those of you who don't know...

John 10:10

"The thief cometh not, but for to steal, and to kill, and to destroy: I am come that they might have life, and that they might have it more abundantly."

1 Peter 5:8

"Be sober, be vigilant; because your adversary the devil, as a roaring lion, walketh about, seeking whom he may devour:"

2 Corinthians 11:14

"And no marvel; for Satan himself is transformed into an angel of light."

Food for thought:

Transparent moment: I hate to hurt your feelings, but Satan hates everything about you. He does not want us to succeed in life at all. So, stop doing **EVERYTHING** that pleases him, which is **ANYTHING** that goes against the word of God. The **ONE** who truly cares, loves, and wants the best for us. You can tell when a situation is starting to go south. Flee from it and "leave well enough alone."

Here are some questions for you to consider:

1. At what age did you realize this Satan character was real?

2. Do you have a problem distinguishing between the voice of God and Satan when told to do something? *(Yes or No)*

3. If so, let your group leader know so he/she can take a moment to pray for you, because it is vital that you listen to the right voice which is God. If you have not received Jesus as your Lord and Savior yet, your group leader can help you with this also. Now would be a great time!

Chapter 13

"It's Okay To Spill The Beans Sometimes"

"Calvin said, 'What's up, Corey? How was your day?' Calvin backed out." (pg. 87)

"'Good,' answered Corey while looking at his dad strangely, 'You sure are in a good mood.' 'Why you say that?' Calvin asked.

'Because you never ask how my day was. Normally, you have that 'It's been a long day.' look on your face,' he told his dad. Then asked, 'Was your day good?'

'My day was great!'

'How, what happened?'

'I…' Calvin thought to himself, 'Maybe I shouldn't tell him about Patrice.' So he answered, 'Got a lot done today in a short amount of time." (pg. 88)

In this case, Calvin should have spilled the beans instead of being secretive about having lunch with Patrice and taking her to the airport. Who knows, telling Corey about it could have held Calvin accountable. And what I mean by this is after telling him, Corey could have convinced his dad to tell his mom which would prevent further problems and nip Satan's agenda right in the butt. When God gave me this dialogue, I could literally see Satan clapping his hands and celebrating when Calvin did not say anything about his discreet lunch date. That is why having a strong relationship with God is really important because He will help you make the right decisions when you just don't know what to say or do in certain situations… or you know what to do, but want to be a knucklehead about it.

The word of God says in…

Proverbs 3:5-6

"Trust in the LORD with all thine heart; and lean not unto thine own understanding. In all thy ways acknowledge him, and he shall direct thy paths."

And then the Lord says…

Psalm 32:8

"I will instruct thee and teach thee in the way which thou shalt go: I will guide thee with mine eye."

Psalm 37:23

"The steps of a good man are ordered by the LORD: and he delighteth in his way."

Food for thought:

It's okay to spill the beans sometimes *if* spilling the beans will help you in becoming a better person or help someone else. At the end of the day, we all must answer to God for our deeds done, good or bad. Just know He sees it all whether you keep things a secret or not.

Here are some questions for you to consider:

1. Have you ever come face-to-face with having to decide whether to tell a secret or not because of what the outcome would be? *(Yes or No)*

2. Whether your answer was yes or no, what was the outcome?

3. Some of you may be familiar with the old saying, "What you don't know, won't hurt you." With your own life experiences and what you have read in the book so far, how do you now feel about this statement?

Chapter 14

"It's Your Mind, Take Control"

"He couldn't seem to get his mind off of his encounter with Patrice. After a while, he got up and left out of his office, heading to Simon's office." (pg. 90)

"'Do you already have someone to head up those projects?'

'Well, I've chosen Paul for it because he doesn't have a family and doesn't mind going. I figured you wouldn't want to be away from your family that long.'

'For how long?' asked Calvin.

'Three weeks… possibly more.'

'That's not bad. And I've been wanting to see what the Dallas office is like anyway.'" (pg. 91)

We can see clearly where Calvin's priority and mind is… certainly not on his family. It seems as though his boss cares more about his family than he does. I don't believe it's intentional, but remember right now, Satan has him hooked, and that is because he *barely* has a relationship with God. So, even his thoughts are now polluted. Let me show you how Satan worked this part and does so with people. Calvin *allowed* the thought to come into his head about Patrice. Then Calvin acted on that thought by initiating the request to his boss to go work in Dallas. And before you knew it, was already emailing Patrice to let her know he was coming without a word to his wife yet about it. Again, if Calvin *knew* God the way that he should, he could have shut that initial thought down and none of this would have gotten as far as it did. How do we keep our mind from being polluted with evil thoughts and under control?

The word of God says in…

Philippians 4:8

"Finally, brethren, whatsoever things are true, whatsoever things are honest, whatsoever things are just, whatsoever things are pure, whatsoever things are lovely, whatsoever things are of good report; if there be any virtue, and if there be any praise, think on these things."

2 Corinthians 10:5

"Casting down imaginations, and every high thing that exalteth itself against the knowledge of God, and bringing into captivity every thought to the obedience of Christ;"

Isaiah 26:3

"Thou wilt keep him in perfect peace, whose mind is stayed on thee: because he trusteth in thee."

Food for thought:

Remember, every action, good or bad, starts as a thought. That is why it is important to fill your mind up with God's word and empty out the lies Satan puts in. That is taking control!

Here are some questions for you to consider:

1. When Satan puts a negative thought into your head, what action do you take?

2. When God tells you to do something, do you act upon it right away? *(Yes or No)* If no, why not. Briefly explain.

3. Which voice do you feel you hear more of, God's or Satan's?

4. In regard to how you answered #3, explain briefly how you know this is the voice you hear more of. For example, "I know I hear the voice of God a lot because He has me give almost every time there's an offering."

Chapter 15

"You Are Not Forgotten"

"David answered his mom, 'Trying to hurry up so Daddy and I can go out to the field today.'

'I almost forgot about that, David,' Calvin said.

'Are we going?'

'Yeah, we'll go out there for a little bit.'

'A little bit? You leave out tomorrow night for three weeks. Can't you spend more than just a little bit with him?' asked Elaina." (pg. 93)

Calvin stated he **almost** forgot about helping David with football. How many of you believe he just plain forgot because his mind was strictly on getting to Dallas? Well, I want you to remember our Father in Heaven will **never** forget you and is always available when you need Him, no matter what or when. He never forgets the promises He made to us, no matter how long they may take to manifest. Your earthly father may and can forget about you, but not your "Daddy" in Heaven. I'm sure some of you might have already experienced this. If so, my heart goes out to you. I read in a devotional recently written by Rick Warren that said, "Your earthly father may not always know what's best, but your Heavenly Father does." That is because there is no greater love than His.

The word of God says in…

1 Corinthians 8:6

"But to us there is but one God, the Father, of whom are all things, and we in him; and one Lord Jesus Christ, by whom are all things, and we by him."

2 Corinthians 6:18

"And will be a Father unto you, and ye shall be my sons and daughters, saith the Lord Almighty."

1 John 3:1

"Behold, what manner of love the Father hath bestowed upon us, that we should be called the sons of God: therefore the world knoweth us not, because it knew him not."

Food for thought:

God, your Heavenly Father, formed your innermost being, shaping your delicate inside and your intricate outside, and wove them all together in your mother's womb *(Psalm 139:13)*. God just used your earthly father to plant you as a seed; however, your Heavenly Father put you together. You belong to Him. So, he's the one that *really* knows **ALL** your *specific* needs, wants, and can actually provide them naturally and spiritually, while your earthly father is limited in this capacity. It is okay to love our earthly fathers and expect some things of and from them, but we must remember… they are not God.

Here are some questions for you to consider:

1. With your earthly father, do you ever feel or have you *ever* felt unloved or forgotten about? *(Yes or No)*   If yes, why?

2. With God, do you ever feel or have you ever felt unloved or forgotten about? *(Yes or No)* If yes, why?

3. At this moment, do you still feel the same way about either one of them OR both? *(Yes or No)* Briefly explain your answer whether it is yes or no.

Chapter 16

"Our Words Shape Our World"

"'There's still a lot of work to be put in, David. I haven't seen enough to show me yet you can make it in the pros; let alone, college.'

'Well, I just have to show you, Pops!' David said. 'That's why I need you there at the game. And I'm still banking on Pastor G putting in a good word for me to the man upstairs.'

'If that's what you still wanna do, David, be my guest,' Calvin said while shaking his head." (pg. 98)

Unfortunately, there are a lot of parents that speak like this to their children causing them to pursue another path in life rather than what God predestined them to do. Thank God David took those words as motivation to prove to his dad that he *will* show him he can make it in the pros and college. However, for a lot of kids, words like that can turn them to the streets, have them dropping out of school, taking drugs… you name it, because the dream that God placed in them has been *shot down* by people that are supposed to *build them up.*

The word of God says in…

Proverbs 18:21

"Death and life are in the power of the tongue: and they that love it shall eat the fruit thereof."

Ephesians 4:29

"Let no corrupt communication proceed out of your mouth, but that which is good to the use of edifying, that it may minister grace unto the hearers."

Matthew 15:18-19

"But those things which proceed out of the mouth come forth from the heart; and they defile the man. For out of the heart proceed evil thoughts, murders, adulteries, fornications, thefts, false witness, blasphemies:"

Food for thought:

We must remember "our words shape our world" whether they are spoken to yourself and/or someone else. Be careful of what you speak.

Here are some questions for you to consider:

1. What does "our words shape our world" mean to you?

2. Have you ever had someone speak against a dream or passion of yours? *(Yes or No)*

3. If so, did you use it as motivation like David did or did you allow it to stop you from accomplishing what God has placed in your heart to do? Briefly explain your answer.

Chapter 17

"Going From Bitter To Better"

Before we get started with this chapter, I want you to find the Lord's Prayer in the The Passion Translation (Matthew 6:9-13). Either write it out or make a copy of it and have it available for an activity at the end of this lesson.

"'He's carrying in a strong bitterness in his heart which is going to backfire against him if he doesn't get rid of it. That's what bitterness does, you know. Who is he angry with?'

'The only person I can think of right now is his dad; even though what happened to him was well over thirty years ago. He's still angry with him and won't let it go.'" (pg. 101)

Out of all the chapters in the "Change of Heart: Never Say Never" novel, this one with Elaina and Mother Newsome, is one of the most important chapters. Why you ask? Because the main focus of the story is about **"forgiveness"**. There are so many people who have been hurt and have not addressed it as they should. So, they are walking around bitter, angry, and/or depressed when all they need to do is just forgive. Is that person you? I didn't say it was easy, and I didn't say you had to forget what happened to you. However, if you want to live out the rest of your days on this earth in peace and have your sanity, then you need to forgive those that have hurt you. Otherwise, Satan will find some way to use the pain you're in to hurt you even more. That is why God *requires* us to forgive so we can live free from Satan's strongholds.

There are a lot of verses in the Bible about forgiveness, but here are a few of my favorite ones…

Mark 11:25

"And when ye stand praying, forgive, if ye have ought against any: that your Father also which is in heaven may forgive you your trespasses."

Ephesians 4:31-32

"Let all bitterness, and wrath, and anger, and clamour, and evil speaking, be put away from you, with all malice: And be ye kind one to another, tenderhearted, forgiving one another, even as God for Christ's sake hath forgiven you."

Hebrews 12:15

"Looking diligently lest any man fail of the grace of God; lest any root of bitterness springing up trouble you, and thereby many be defiled;"

Food for thought:

If it makes you feel better about forgiving the person that hurt you, just know forgiveness is for **YOU**, not for the abuser, offender, or whomever hurt you. If you don't want to live a life of being Satan's puppet, then you need to learn how to forgive. If not, then that is what you will become… if you are not that already. God made **YOU** "better" than that. You need to know also that unforgiveness can bring about sickness upon your body, prevent you from being healed of sickness, or hold up your blessings. Sounds like the work of Satan to me. Therefore, you need to forgive!

Here are some questions for you to consider:

1. Time to really dig into this forgiveness thing. Are you still angry or bitter at someone who hurt you recently or in the past? *(Yes or No)* Be honest…

2. If yes, are you finding it hard to forgive them? *(Yes or No)*

3. If yes, now is a great time to go from bitter to better. As Mother Newsome said, "It's not good to carry mess like that to your grave." *(pg. 102)* Tomorrow is not promised, no matter what age you are. And if you said no, you can still do this, just in case you forgot someone.

Here is an activity for you! Be sure to read through all the instructions before you get started.

1. Bring out that copy of the Lord's Prayer that I wanted you to either write down or make a copy of.

2. Find a quiet secluded area if you are working on this study by yourself *(you may already be there)*. If you are in a group, give yourselves some space between each other.

3. Now, think about the name(s) of those in your head that you are still angry or bitter with.

4. Begin to speak the Lord's Prayer, and when you get to verse 12, I want you to make it personal. And where it says, "release forgiveness to those", fill in the word "those" with the actual names you are bitter or angry with. So, it should go like this, "Forgive <u>me</u> the wrongs I have done as <u>I, myself</u> release forgiveness to _____ who have wronged <u>me</u>."

Chapter 18

"Surprise, Surprise"

"'But I haven't done anything, T.B.!' Calvin asserted. 'Are you gonna tell Laina about this?' Tony didn't answer right away. He finally said, 'I don't know. I may not have to. Things have a way of being exposed, you know.'" (pg. 109)

Wow, there is so much going on in this chapter, especially things that should not be. Wouldn't you agree? I'm sure Patrice nor Calvin thought T.B., out of all people, would show up at that time. When you think you're getting away with something because you're not seen, God sees and knows EVERYTHING you do. Although T.B. wasn't sure if he was going to tell Elaina or not about seeing Calvin, it would eventually come out and "expose" exactly the wrong that he's been doing. Nothing is coincidental. **Exposing your wrong is right** and will only make you into a better person and draw you closer to the God.

The word of God says in…

Ephesians 5:11-13

"And have no fellowship with the unfruitful works of darkness, but rather reprove them. For it is a shame even to speak of those things which are done of them in secret. But all things that are reproved are made manifest by the light: for whatsoever doth make manifest is light."

John 3:20

"For every one that doeth evil hateth the light, neither cometh to the light, lest his deeds should be reproved."

1 Corinthians 4:5

"Therefore judge nothing before the time, until the Lord come, who both will bring to light the hidden things of darkness, and will make manifest the counsels of the hearts: and then shall every man have praise of God."

Food for thought:

If you don't feel like you're progressing in life like you should be, ask God to expose or reveal any areas in your life that need to be rectified. And when you take action to fix whatever flaws He shows you, that is when you will see God move in a mighty way upon your life like never before.

Here are some questions for you to consider:

1. Have you ever been in a situation in your life *(as a child or as an adult)* where you were exposed? *(Yes or No)* Be honest.

2. If yes, which everyone should have said yes because "nobody is perfect" remember, briefly explain what happened.

3. If you came upon this situation all over again, what would you have done differently?

Chapter 19

"Are You Ready For Some Football?"

"Among the pumped up crowd was David's fan club which consisted of Elaina, Corey, Katrina, Michelle and Darren. They were all standing, blowing each other's ears out as they cheered for David running with the football." (pg. 113)

"David crossed the goal line for a touchdown as anticipated and did a quick celebration with a few teammates while in the end zone." (pg. 113)

It's game time!!! David is certainly proving to not only his dad, who is absent from this important game, but to everyone in the stands, his team, and his opponents that he can make it to the next level. That next level for him is college..

So, let's have a little fun and play a game called "The College Mascot Challenge"! This can be played individually or as a group. If playing as a group, make it even more exciting by giving a prize to the person who has the highest score.

Here are the instructions:

1. Open up a browser on one of your devices and type in The College Mascot Challenge. This game is by How Stuff Works. Click on it.

2. You will see an orange button that says "Read More" which you may click on to learn more about this challenge, or you can go ahead and start the challenge. DO NOT PRESS "HINT" UNLESS YOUR GROUP LEADER SAY YOU CAN OR TELL YOU HOW MANY QUESTIONS YOU ARE ALLOWED TO PRESS THE "HINT" BUTTON FOR.

3. After you finish answering the questions, you will see how you stack up!

Have fun!

Chapter 20

"Don't Forget To Give Thanks"

"At the kitchen table, Elaina relaxed with a hot cup of lemon and honey tea to soothe her voice from all of the shouting she did at the game, as she reflected upon how well her son did. She had a smile of gratitude on her face as she stared at her cup. She said, 'Thank you Lord, for what you did tonight with David.'" (pg. 117)

I love the fact that Elaina realizes that David could not have done what he did in the game if it wasn't for the Lord. Jesus, our Lord and Savior, is how we are able to carry out our gift(s) and talent(s). And God, the Father of Jesus, is the author of these gift(s) and talent(s). We must never forget that nor take them for granted. So, it is important to give thanks every chance we get.

The word of God says in…

John 15:5

"I am the vine, ye are the branches: He that abideth in me, and I in him, the same bringeth forth much fruit: for without me ye can do nothing."

The word of God also says…

James 1:17-18

"Every good gift and every perfect gift is from above, and cometh down from the Father of lights, with whom is no variableness, neither shadow of turning. Of his own will begat he us with the word of truth, that we should be a kind of firstfruits of his creatures."

Philippians 2:13

"For it is God which worketh in you both to will and to do of his good pleasure."

Food for thought:

The moment you think you have arrived and you believe you are doing great works on your own, God will give you a reminder by sitting you down. So, do yourself a favor… stay humble and thank the Lord with every opportunity you get for helping you perform every great work. The more praises go up, the less arrogant you become.

Here are some questions for you to consider:

1. Has there ever been an instance where you knew without a doubt it was the Lord that got you through performing a great work? Briefly explain.

2. We live in a world where people believe they are responsible for everything in their lives. They trust more in their education, training, and/or talent(s). Have you ever fell into this trap before? *(Yes or No)* And if so, briefly explain.

Chapter 21

"How Many Signs Do You Need?"

"She opened the door and snuck in a kiss on Calvin's lips as he began walking out of the door. Calvin was without words. 'I'm sorry. I shouldn't have done that,' she said, acting like she was embarrassed by her actions. 'I guess I just really enjoyed your company this evening. It's been a long time since I've had that.'

'I… better go before I find myself doing something I shouldn't. See you tomorrow… at the office.' He quickly exited her apartment." (pg. 121)

You would think Calvin would be trying to avoid seeing Patrice the next day after that; however, that is not the case. He even said, **"I… better go before I find myself doing something I shouldn't."** I'm thinking how many signs does he need to see before he recognizes that he's going down the wrong path? God constantly shows us signs when to run from a trap Satan has set up for us. We, on the other hand, **must** recognize them. The only way to do that is to constantly seek direction from Him in all you do. People have been quick to blame God for bad situations or circumstances they got into. However, if they take a moment and think back, they will quickly realize that God gave them plenty of signs on what to do. They were just ignored or brushed off.

The word of God says in…

Proverbs 3:5-6

"Trust in the LORD with all thine heart; and lean not unto thine own understanding. In all thy ways acknowledge him, and he shall direct thy paths."

Proverbs 16:9

"A man's heart deviseth his way: but the LORD directeth his steps."

Psalm 32:8-9

"I will instruct thee and teach thee in the way which thou shalt go: I will guide thee with mine eye."

Food for thought:

Some of the signs God gives are BIG and some are subtle. At any rate, big or subtle, you will begin to see them clearly as you spend more time with God and in His word.

Here are some questions for you to consider:

1. Take a moment now and think back to when you were in a bad situation or circumstance. Looking back, do you believe God gave you signs that would have prevented you from ever getting into *that* situation or circumstance, but you ignored them or brushed them off? *(Yes or No)*

2. If yes, write those sign(s) down if you can remember them.

3. Were the sign(s) big, subtle, or both?

4. Had you recognized them at the time shown, what would you have done differently?

Chapter 22

"You Are Being Watched By Somebody"

"'That's Patrice!' Elaina exclaimed." (pg. 124)

"Michelle flipped her phone back around to her. 'You know her?'

'Yeah. I met her when she and Tony came to Calvin's company fall festival. She works for the same company Calvin does,' Elaina responded with bewilderment.

'You talking about Calvin's friend, Tony?'

'Yeah. Tony and Calvin met her at Jay's Lounge.'

Michelle said, 'She came to the salon to get her hair done some weeks ago. She's a client of my friend, April. I should've known she was trouble then. You want me to take the phone over there?' Michelle asked.

'No, Michelle. I'll handle it. I'll talk to you later.'

Michelle replied, 'Alright.' She hung up with her sister and continued eating." (pg. 125)

An opportune time doesn't always mean it's a good time to take action. Elaina and Michelle handled that moment well. I believe because Elaina didn't flip out at that moment, her sister didn't. Michelle is not as saved as Elaina, if at all. So, she could have easily acted a fool. As believers, our actions are always being watched by others, especially family. Most of the time, it is our family members who are the most judgmental. While that may be the case, we still must remember that we are to be a light in darkness because you never know who is watching and who's life depends on seeing your light. You never know who is on the fence between following Christ or not.

The word of God says in…

Matthew 5:14-16

"Ye are the light of the world. A city that is set on a hill cannot be hid. Neither do men light a candle, and put it under a bushel, but on a candlestick; and it giveth light unto all that are in the house. Let your light so shine before men, that they may see your good works, and glorify your Father which is in heaven."

Ephesians 5:8-9

"For ye were sometimes darkness, but now are ye light in the Lord: walk as children of light: (For the fruit of the Spirit is in all goodness and righteousness and truth;)."

Food for thought:

For this food for thought, I'm going to share a personal testimony. Some years ago in Tampa, FL at a doctor's office I worked at, a young lady several years younger than I, watched me while working there. We were not close friends, but we got along really well. And from time to time, I would encourage, pray with her, and give her Godly counsel when needed. During my tenure at this office, I was a believer but not at the level of where I am today. After some years of working there with this young lady, I left that company and pursued a different career path, eventually moving out of the state to Nashville, TN. About five or so years later, this young lady called to tell me "thank you" for changing her life and that she watched me. She told me how she was a Christian and doing full-time ministry with her husband who was a minister. She wasn't married when we worked together and was a single mom with the life of a roller coaster. I began to cry, and my heart was overjoyed because I never knew this young lady was watching me until she called.

Here are some questions for you to consider:

1. What does 'being a light in darkness' mean to you?

2. What are 2-3 things you do to exemplify your light to others in the world?

3. Has *your* light ever led someone to Christ for which you found out about it later on in life? *(Yes or No)*

If so, way to go!!!

Chapter 23

"Now What?"

"'Okay, God, now what? You said you work all things out for our good. How are you going to work this one out? Sometimes you're loud and clear… this time, you're quiet,' she told God. 'I don't even know what to pray right now. I'm so angry with him,' she said to herself. 'Convict him… please convict him! Help him to see what he's doing is wrong. It's wrong! Lord, just hurry and bring him back home where he needs to be,' prayed Elaina with tears in her eyes." (pg. 132)

Sometimes we are hit so hard with hurt that we need to pray but don't know what to pray or do. When you have exhausted all your options, without losing hope, you hold to the last ounce of word you have inside of you. And trust that God hears your every cry, even when you don't hear His voice.

The word of God says in…

Psalms 34:17

"The righteous cry, and the LORD heareth, and delivereth them out of all their troubles."

Psalms 145:19

"He will fulfil the desire of them that fear him: he also will hear their cry, and will save them."

1 Peter 3:12

"For the eyes of the Lord are over the righteous, and his ears are open unto their prayers: but the face of the Lord is against them that do evil."

Food for thought:

When you're at the point where you don't know what to pray anymore, find scripture that relates to your situation or circumstance and pray the word. God hears you and is fighting your battles for you, even when you can't tell or see it. Our timetable is not His timetable; however, His timing is always perfect.

Here are some questions for you to consider:

1. Have you ever gotten to a point like Elaina, where you did not know what to pray anymore or not pray at all? *(Yes or No)*

2. If so, what did you do? Briefly explain.

3. What was the outcome? Briefly explain.

4. Knowing what you know now, what would you do differently than before? Briefly explain.

Chapter 24

"Wolves In Sheep's Clothing"

"'Yep, I can't wait for him to come home,' Corey answered while taking a few sips of his water. Then, he looked at Darren with a mystified expression before the thought of his dad came to mind. 'I miss him,' Corey said.

Darren placed his hand on Corey's leg. 'I'm sure you do, Corey. I kind of fill in as a dad for some of the guys at the center who dads are not around.'" (pg. 135)

Well, you've read this chapter and can clearly see what is taking place. I hate to say it, but yes, there are even family members or people we call family who are wolves in sheep's clothing. As my own testimony, I have experienced this and thus my reason for doing the book and movie. I did not understand for a long time how God would give someone who did not go to film school, a film, nor have ever written a book, a book. It wasn't until 2017 after attending a retreat that my church, World Harvest Church of Roswell, does called The Encounter, that I received revelation as to why God gave me all of this to do. It was because He knew that I needed to forgive the family members that molested me so that I could help others in the world do the same. And just like Corey, I trusted the very ones that were close to me and could not fathom the reason for their strange behavior towards me. However, now as an adult, I understand the force that contributed to it. I'm so glad God gives beauty for ashes. Be careful of wolves in sheep's clothing!

The word of God says in…

Romans 16:17-18

"Now I beseech you, brethren, mark them which cause divisions and offences contrary to the doctrine which ye have learned; and avoid them."

Acts 20:29

"For I know this, that after my departing shall grievous wolves enter among you, not sparing the flock."

Luke 10:3

"Go your ways: behold, I send you forth as lambs among wolves."

Food for thought:

As much as I try to keep those incidents out of my head, every now and then, they still pop up. That is nobody but Satan trying to distract me; however, the Holy Spirit always reminds me that I am no longer bound, and those incidents does not define who I am. Then those horrible visions go away, and I keep it moving. I believe I'm able to do this *only* because I succumbed to forgiving those family members who violated me. I'm also careful to recognize wolves in sheep's clothing now with the gift of discernment given by the Holy Spirit. You can do the same!

Here are some questions for you to consider:

1. Has anyone ever appeared to you as a wolf in sheep's clothing? *(Yes or No)*

2. If so, what did you do when you found out what they were really all about?

3. Have you forgiven them? *(Yes or No)*

If you still find it hard to do so, hopefully by the time you get to the end of working this study guide, you will have done so. Again, God's desire is for you to live in peace and free from Satan's strongholds.

Chapter 25

"It's Not You"

"'God, am I being punished for something I did? What did I do wrong?' asked Corey. 'He's supposed to be family! What kind of family does that?' Corey quickly wiped his face when he heard a knock at his door." (pg. 142)

I mentioned in the introduction that I'm sure each of you can relate to at least one of the characters in the novel. For me, I relate to both Elaina *(as a parent)* and Corey *(as a child)*. Elaina could have decided not to believe Corey because of her and Darren's relationship, but as you can see, she took him seriously. In most cases, that does not happen because the victim feels no one will believe them or they don't want to cause chaos within their circle. It's unfortunate that most people *(young child, teenager or adult)* who has been molested or abused in some form or fashion, believe they have done something wrong as to the reason they were or are being treated unjustly. Let me tell you... this is *far* from the truth and a lie from the pit of hell. God's desire is for us to LOVE one another. Some choices we make *can* put us in bad situations sometimes; however, any type of immoral behavior is wrong and is not love. God's will is for us to be whole, healthy, and prosperous.

The word of God says in...

Jeremiah 29:11

"For I know the thoughts that I think toward you, saith the LORD, thoughts of peace, and not of evil, to give you an expected end."

3 John 1:2

"Beloved, I wish above all things that thou mayest prosper and be in health, even as thy soul prospereth."

Galatians 5:13-14

"For, brethren ye have been called unto liberty; only use not liberty for an occasion to the flesh, but by love serve one another. For all the law is fulfilled in one word, even in this; Thou shalt love thy neighbour as thyself."

Food for thought:

No one has the right to place their hands on you inappropriately, whether sexually or domestically. If you have found yourself in any of these situations, rest assured, you did nothing wrong. However, I encourage you to speak to someone you know is trustworthy, especially if you are currently in that situation. And if you don't have anyone, contact the phone number listed at the end of this study. God will give you strength to speak up if you ask Him to. Although late in life, He did it for me in 2017 when He gave me the courage to tell my parents. It wasn't easy, but I did it. You can too!

Here are some questions for you to consider:

1. Do you feel you are being punished when bad things happen to you? *(Yes or No)*

2. If yes, why do you feel that way? Briefly explain.

3. What do you think would change how you feel about that, if you answered yes?

***If you need someone to talk to regarding sexual abuse, you can call the National Sexual Assault Telephone Hotline at (800)656-HOPE (4673). For domestic abuse, you can call the National Domestic Violence Hotline at (800)799-SAFE (7233) Remember, it's okay to "spill the beans." ***

Chapter 26

"Man Up"

"The officer read Darren his rights as he took out his handcuffs. He had Darren turn around and then he cuffed him. He pulled Darren to the side to speak with him further and then told the other two officers to go inside of Darren's home to do a search. Darren didn't hold back on giving any information. It was almost like he was ready to be caught." (pg. 148)

Not to excuse what Darren is doing; however, most of the time, there is a root cause that drives one's immoral behavior. We already know it is demonic; however, history can be repeating itself unfortunately. We will discuss this more in detail at a later time. Now, back to the point of it being demonic… it may appear that Darren was ready to give up this vicious cycle of immoral behavior, who knows. At any rate, I believe there are quite a few people walking around with all kinds of demons who are silently crying out for help and hoping to be rescued from them but don't know how to break away. Demonic forces are real and serve to complete Satan's work on the earth. And if your inner man is not strong enough to ward them off, they will surely take control of your mind, body, and soul. Satan and his imps do not fight fair. So, you must *"Man Up"* to him and not allow him to take control.

The word of God says in…

1 Timothy 4:1-2

"Now the Spirit speaketh expressly, that in the latter times some shall depart from the faith, giving heed to seducing spirits, and doctrines of devils; Speaking lies in hypocrisy; having their conscience seared with a hot iron;"

Matthew 12:43-45

"When the unclean spirit is gone out of a man, he walketh through dry places, seeking rest, and findeth none Then he saith, I will return into my house from whence I came out; and when he is come, he findeth it empty, swept, and garnished. Then goeth he, and taketh with himself seven other spirits more wicked than himself, and they enter in and dwell there: and the last state of that man is worse than the first. Even so shall it be also unto this wicked generation."

Ephesians 6:10-12

"Finally, my brethren, be strong in the Lord, and in the power of his might. Put on the whole armour of God, that ye may be able to stand against the wiles of the devil. For we wrestle not against flesh and blood, but against principalities, against spiritual wickedness in high places."

Food for thought:

The more you feed your spirit man with spiritual food *(God's word)*, the more power you will have to battle in the spirit when being attacked.

Here are some questions for you to consider:

1. Name two things you do to war in the spirit when being attacked?

2. We all know the year of 2020 was a rough year with one huge major attack, specifically speaking, COVID-19. In addition to surviving this global pandemic, I'm sure each of you have had your own spiritual warfare to battle personally. List 2-3 battles you won in 2020 that Satan tried to defeat you with.

If you listed any, use these as a reminder when you feel you cannot break away from an attack. Remember "greater is He in you than he that is in the world." *(1 John 4:4)* **So Man Up!!**

Chapter 27

"Whatever It Takes"

"He wandered around in his bedroom with his hands interlocked behind his head for a few moments, before he sat back down on the side of the bed and raised his head toward the ceiling. 'God… I'm really not good at this praying thing. Never have been… but… I know this is all my fault. Corey's a good kid and didn't deserve this.' He stared at the wall in front of him. He said to himself, 'What am I doing here? Maybe Laina was right.' He raised his head back up to the ceiling and said, 'Whatever it takes God… I'll do it.'" (pg. 154-155)

Finally, Calvin took God off the shelf! It is sad that many believers, like Calvin, don't pray or talk to God until something bad happens. Had he been talking to Him from the very moment he had the encounter with Patrice, I don't believe things would have gotten as far as they did. You will save yourself a lot of heartache in life if you just consult God from the get-go. The statement, "Whatever it takes God… I'll do it.", should be everyone's confession constantly; not when we're facing a tragedy. And again, aside from Him, we are nothing. This is what you call humility.

The word of God says…

Proverbs 11:2

"When pride cometh, then cometh shame: but with the lowly is wisdom."

Proverbs 22:4

"By humility and the fear of the LORD are riches, and honour, and life."

James 3:2

"For in many things we offend all. If any man offend not in word, the same is a perfect man, and able also to bridle the whole body."

Food for thought:

Humility is not a sign of weakness as some people may think. It is a sign of strength and will keep you grounded in life. When you're full of yourself, there's no room left for God to move as He desires to do inside and through you.

Here are some questions for you to consider:

1. Have you ever been at that place like Calvin, where you have or had reached the end of your rope, and you cried out to God like never before? *(Yes or No)*

2. What was the outcome of your surrender to God? Briefly explain.

3. If you could do it all over again, would you wait and allow circumstances to push you to surrender to God or would you just do it out of your own free will? Briefly explain.

Chapter 28

"He's Working It Out For Your Good"

"Calvin said, 'Laina… I asked Simon to go to Dallas. But only after a little persuasion.' David and Katrina looked at each other when they heard that. Elaina just said, 'Hmm, hmm…' Elaina said to herself, 'Keep talking, negro.'

'I lied to you when you asked me who I ate with at the restaurant the other night.'

Elaina just said, 'Hmm, hmm…' Again, she was saying to herself, 'Keep going', as she folded her arms." (pg. 160)

"'I had dinner with Patrice that night and the night before…' Elaina's mouth dropped open slightly as she cocked her head to the side, surprised at what Calvin just told her. David and Katrina again looked at each other on the other side of the wall. Calvin quickly said, 'But nothing further happened. It was just dinner… I promise.'

'I know. Well, correction… I knew about dinner at the restaurant… not about the one you had before,' Elaina explained. Then said, 'Michelle happened to be in Dallas for a hair show and was eating at that same restaurant when she saw you with her.'" (pg. 161)

Wow, look at that… Calvin spilled the beans and then some. So, it turns out that his best friend, T.B., did not have to say a word to Elaina. Calvin was convicted enough to tell everything. Needless to say, Elaina's prayer was answered. It took complete trust on her part. That's hard to do in a situation like this, but essential. When you put your complete trust in the Lord, your situation will always work out for your good and much better than how you would have handled it.

The word of God says in…

Proverbs 3:5-6

"Trust in the LORD with all thine heart; and lean not unto thine own understanding. In all thy ways acknowledge him, and he shall direct thy paths."

Psalm 118:8

"It is better to trust in the LORD than to put confidence in princes."

Romans 8:28

"And we know that all things work together for good to them that love God, to them who are the called according to his purpose."

Food for thought:

If you haven't seen your answer(s) manifest yet, don't give up! You're one prayer away from your answer(s). Even if you have to pray grinding your teeth or crying… don't stop. The Lord *really* is working all things out for your good, which will unfold <u>only</u> if you put your complete trust in Him.

Here are some questions for you to consider:

1. Are you currently in an odd situation now, where you are waiting for the Lord to still answer your prayer(s)? *(Yes or No)*

2. If yes, how long have you been waiting?

3. Have you put your complete trust in the Lord regarding this situation? *(Yes or No)* Be honest…

4. What does "complete trust in the Lord" mean to you? Briefly explain.

Chapter 29

"Forgiveness Is The Key"

"'I had to learn the hard way that it's not good to hold on to past hurt. I almost fell in the same trap that caused my hurt. It not only tortures you, but also those around you. So… I'm doing this for myself and my family.' explained Calvin. He focused his attention on Corey specifically. 'I can't help them, if I'm not right myself,' Calvin said to him." (pg. 164)

"Calvin said to the congregation, 'Today, I can truly say, I forgive my dad when I thought I never would. Because I, for the first time, felt what it was like to need forgiving. Now I know what my mom was talking about when she told me God gives us mercy over and over again, even when we do wrong." (Pg. 165)

Finally, Calvin surrenders! The "dead weight" that Pastor Gillesby is referring to in this chapter on page 164 is nothing more than a stronghold birthed with the help of Satan. The only remedy for lifting that weight was for him to **forgive** his dad. Now, he has complete freedom and peace in that area and can help his son learn how to do the same. Getting over a tremendous hurt can *only* be overcome with the Lord's help. **Forgiveness** is the *key* to unlock that locked area of your heart that has been wounded. Then and only then, can the Lord go in and repair that wound. You have seen forgiveness mentioned in a few chapters back. And we will continue to discuss this because it is the meat of this story and the hardest for people to do; however, *must* be done.

The word of God says in…

Psalm 147:3

"He health the broken in heart, and bindeth up their wounds."

In Matthew 11:28   The Lord says…

"Come unto me, all ye that labour and are heavy laden, and I will give you rest."

Philippians 4:6-7

"Be careful for nothing; but in every thing by prayer and supplication with thanksgiving let your requests be made known unto God."

Food for thought:

I cannot begin to tell you how it felt when my weight was lifted and the wound in my heart was repaired. It was a weight I did not know I even had until I had my own heart-2-heart with God. This was hurt carried since I was a little girl and thought for sure I had gotten over it and had forgiven until I opened my heart completely to God. With every hurt, make sure you do the same.

Here are some questions for you to consider:

1. You are at the point where you have gone through quite a few lessons in this study guide and are now here in this lesson. Have you discovered any area(s) of your heart that is still wounded, and you're struggling to overcome? *(Yes or No)*

2. If yes, why do you feel it is still a struggle to overcome? Briefly explain.

3. If no, did you have any before you started this study guide? *(Yes or No)*

4. If yes, what did you do to receive your breakthrough? And at what point in the study guide did you receive it? Briefly explain, and then maybe share your process to those in your group who are still struggling to overcome their hurt, if you are comfortable with doing so.

Chapter 30

"Game On"

"The stands were completely filled with Eagles fans and Tigers fans. Almost everyone was on their feet screaming. With David's size and speed, the Eagles' players were finding it difficult to bring him down." (Pg. 166)

"Calvin shouted 'There it is, son!' toward the field as David crossed the goal line. Then, he announced out loud to the crowd, 'That's my boy!' hoping everyone around him heard that. Well it certainly didn't go unnoticed." (pg. 167)

It was "game on" again for David, and now it's "game on" again for you!!! However, first, a few comments… This time, David got a chance to put on a show for the one he's been trying to impress all along… his dad. Needless to say, his dad finally took notice and made sure everyone knew that David belonged to him. Most of the time, boys are always trying to impress their fathers, and sometimes daughters will even do the same. This is how it should be for our Heavenly Father. It should *always* be "game on" for His sons and daughters, constantly working at impressing Him and winning in life.

So, let's see how well you do at impressing our Heavenly Father with this game called "Do You Know Your Bible Trivia Backward and Forward?"! This can be played individually or as a group. If playing as a group, make it even more exciting by giving a prize to the person who has the highest score.

1. Open up a browser on one of your devices and type in Do You Know Your Bible Trivia Backward and Forward. This game is by How Stuff Works. Click on it.

2. You will see an orange button that says "Read More" which you may click on to learn more about this challenge, or you can go ahead and start the challenge. You can play this game as an individual or group. For this game, you can use your Bible or not. You can use the "Hint" buttons or not. I'll leave that up to your group leader; however, if you really want to impress Daddy in Heaven, don't you use it.

3. After you finish answering the questions, you will see just how well you impressed Him. I think I did pretty well. I used my Bible once on one question and got one wrong on another question. Your turn!

Game On!

Chapter 31

"Everyone Is Entitled To A Clean Slate"

"'Hi, Junior,' said Calvin Sr. 'Glad you could make it.' Calvin told his dad. Then said, 'Well, come in… come in.' When he stepped inside of the house, Calvin quickly gave him a hug before his dad took off his jacket and fedora, revealing his salt and pepper colored hair. 'Here, let me take your jacket and hat,' he said to his dad, and then hung his jacket and hat on the coat rack. 'Thanks for having me,' said Calvin Sr." (pg. 174)

"No one had met him yet, and Calvin had only been communicating with him over the phone for the past couple of weeks. He announced, 'Everyone… this is my dad, Calvin Hardy Sr.' Elaina stood up, walked over to him and gave him a hug. She said, 'Welcome, Dad. We've been saving a seat just for you.'" (pg. 175)

What a great moment of reconciliation that took place between Calvin and his dad! My absolute favorite moment is when Elaina says, "Welcome, Dad. We've been saving a seat just for you." This reminded me of the prodigal son parable in the book of Luke 15:11-32; however, instead in this case, the son is the one that is receiving his dad back into his life. Sometimes after forgiving, reconciliation may be the next step. That can be just as hard as forgiving, depending on the situation or circumstance. In this case, I believe reconciliation was essential. This is what God does for us when we have sinned and ask for forgiveness. He puts us back in right standing with Him, giving us a clean slate. This is what Calvin did for his dad.

Here's what the word of God says about reconciliation…

2 Corinthians 5:18-19

"And all things are of God, who hath reconciled us to himself by Jesus Christ, and hath given to us the ministry of reconciliation; To wit, that God was in Christ, reconciling the world unto himself, not imputing their trespasses unto them; and hath committed unto us the word of reconciliation."

Romans 5:10

"For if, when we were enemies, we were reconciled to God by the death of his Son, much more, being reconciled, we shall be saved by his life."

Food for thought:

Remember, everyone is entitled to a clean slate whether it's deserved or not. When we sin and fall short of the glory of God *(Romans 3:23)*, thank God He doesn't hold what we do over our heads forever like some people do. So, if you have sinned or someone has sinned against you, He grants a clean slate to each of you. So, stop feeling guilty every time Satan tries to bring up what you did. If you have already repented for your sin(s), you are no longer condemned *(Romans 8:1)*. And as far as someone sinning against you, you just do your part and forgive without holding their sin(s) over their heads. Then let God to do His part.

Here are some questions for you to consider:

1. If you have asked God for forgiveness of your sin(s), does guilt still come upon you or is it constantly thrown back up in your face by others? *(Yes or No)*

2. If so, briefly explain.

3. When this happens, what do you do?

Chapter 32

"The Past Is The Past"

"'As I was saying, Dad… I've come to accept that the past is just that. We can't change what happened, but we can learn from our mistakes and move forward,' explained Calvin." (pg. 179)

Calvin is 100% correct. You cannot change the bad that has happened in your past. You learn from it and move forward. This is easier said than done sometimes; however, as you come to know the Lord more, moving forward will be a piece of cake. How do I know this, you ask? Because as you study the word of God, you will realize who you are, who you belong to, and see that He wants you to conquer in every problematic area of your life. Especially those areas where Satan is trying to bring you down in, and as mentioned in Chapter 31, constantly throw your past up in your face. And another reason I know is because I would never tell you to do something I do not do or have not experienced myself.

The word of God says in…

Isaiah 43:18-19

"Remember ye not the former things, neither consider the things of old. Behold, I will do a new thing; now it shall spring forth; shall ye not know it? I will even make a way in the wilderness, and rivers in the desert."

2 Corinthians 5:17

"Therefore if any man be in Christ, he is a new creature: old things are passed away; behold, all things are become new."

Hebrews 12:1-2

"Wherefore seeing we also are compassed about with so great a cloud of witnesses, let us lay aside every weight, and the sin which doth so easily beset us, and let us run with patience the race that is set before us, Looking unto Jesus the author and finisher of our faith; who for the joy that was set before him endured the cross, despising the shame, and is set down at the right hand of the throne of God."

Food for thought:

Don't define your future by what your past looked like. If the Lord is in you and you in Him *(John 14:20)*, your future looks much brighter than your past. Don't look back at it if you're doing so from guilt and shame, but only as a testimony of where God has brought you from and is taking you now.

Here are some questions for you to consider:

1. What are two things you hated about your past the most?

2. What have you done to change those two things you hated about your past?

3. At this present time, are you satisfied with your change(s)? *(Yes or No)*

4. If not, what do you feel you need to do to make it better? And how will you accomplish this? Briefly explain.

Chapter 33

"That Friend"

"'T.B., wait… I'm calling to say sorry, man. I didn't mean for any of this to happen,' Calvin explained. 'I admit… I got caught up, but nothing happened between us.'" (pg. 183)

"'I just didn't think it would be a problem at the time,' Calvin said. 'Now I know it was a problem from the moment I went to the cafeteria with her.'

'Uh… you think, C.J.?'" (pg. 184)

"'Man, you know we been through too much to let a female come in between us,' he told Calvin. 'And you know, you don't have any other friends really.' Calvin just laughed." (pg. 186)

Certain friendships are gold and should not be traded for anything. Calvin and T.B. both grew up in church and have been there for each other most of their lives. T.B.'s true relationship with God started before Calvin's. And as we saw some chapters back, he was trying his hardest to hold Calvin accountable for his behavior, not only with Patrice, but with his dad as well. Now that Calvin is coming into a true relationship with God also, they can hold each other accountable to make sure they both stay grounded and doing the will of God for their lives. Those are the type of friendships you want and need. God knows what He is doing when he brings people in your life like T.B. You need to cherish this type of friendship. Who is "that friend" for you?

Here's what the word of God says about friendships…

Proverbs 17:17

"A friend loveth at all times, and a brother is born for adversity."

Proverbs 22:24-25

"Make no friendship with an angry man; and with a furious man thou shalt not go: Lest thou learn his ways, and get a snare to thy soul."

Ecclesiastes 4:9-10

"Two are better than one; because they have a good reward for their labour. For if they fall, the one will lift up his fellow: but woe to him that is alone when he falleth; for he hath not another to help him up."

Food for thought:

Friends are wonderful to have; however, you must know there is no friend greater than one who will lay down their life for you. "That friend" for sure, is none other than Jesus, our Lord and Savior. People can become flaky and change at any time. Jesus, however, is the same today, yesterday, and forever more.

Here are some questions for you to consider:

1. Have you ever had to be frank with a friend that needed to be held accountable for something drastic they did or were getting ready to do? *(Yes or No)*

2. How did they react when you told them, if you told them? Briefly explain.

3. If you did not tell them, why not? Briefly explain.

4. Do you have a friend that holds you accountable and will tell you the truth no matter what it is? *(Yes or No)*

5. If so, how do you react when they hold you accountable? Do you get mad at them or receive what they tell you? Briefly explain.

Chapter 34

"You Got This!"

"'No, I better not, Patrice,' he told her. 'I actually shouldn't have joined you when I did before, I shouldn't have taken you to the airport without telling my wife, and I really didn't have any business going to Dallas like I did.'

Patrice turned her head sideways at Calvin as she looked perplexed. 'What are you saying?' asked Patrice, as she sat down in one of his chairs in front of his desk.

'I'm saying, I love my wife, and I want my wife to continue loving me. So our relationship will be strictly business." (pg. 190)

"'Patrice, you're a beautiful woman, but you're not worth losing my family over… at least not for me.'

He sat back in his chair and then turned around to the window facing downtown as he focused his attention outside. He smiled as he said to himself, 'Way to handle that, Calvin.'" (pg. 191)

How about that? Calvin won this battle with Satan! Once you get over one hurdle, it does not mean that Satan is going to stop his tricks and schemes. He's going to push harder, especially as you draw closer to God. And so, we must push even harder back at him by using the tools God gave you… your mouth and His word. You got this!

Here are a few verses to show you exactly what to do to fight back…

James 4:7

"Submit yourselves therefore to God. Resist the devil, and he will flee from you."

Ephesians 6:11-18

"Put on the whole armour of God, that ye may be able to stand against the wiles of the devil. For we wrestle not against flesh and blood, but against principalities, against powers, against the rulers of the darkness of this world, against spiritual wickedness in high places. Wherefore take unto you the whole armour of God, that ye may be able to withstand in the evil day, and having done all, to stand. Stand therefore, having your loins girt about with truth, and having on the breastplate of righteousness; And your feet shod with the preparation of the gospel of peace; Above all, taking the shield of faith, wherewith ye shall be able to quench all the fiery darts of the wicked. And take the helmet of salvation, and the sword of the Spirit, which is the word of God: Praying always with all prayer and supplication in the Spirit, and watching thereunto with all perseverance and supplication for all saints;"

Food for thought:

Look… you have to get downright ugly when it comes to fighting Satan. I've had to learn this myself. I've come to realize that God's word is truly a weapon. And just as you *pray* the word to God; use it as a weapon and *speak* it against Satan. My favorite "bullet" used against Satan is James 4:7. Try it if you haven't already.

Here are some questions for you to consider:

1. Just as God uses people to do His work, Satan uses people to do his as well. Give an example in your life where you have seen this to be evident with Satan.

2. I told you my favorite bullet I like to use against Satan is James 4:7. What is yours? Share with your group. And if you do not have one, now is a great time to get one.

Chapter 35

"A Little Compassion Goes A Long Way"

"'Darren is going to be sentenced on next Friday. The victims can come and say something if they want. Your dad and I will be going. Did you want to go?' Corey stood there for a moment, pondering if he should go or not. Elaina said, 'Sweetheart, you don't have to go if you don't want to. I figured I'd let you make your own decision.' She could already tell he didn't want to." (pg. 194)

"Yeah… I'm not ready to face him again yet.'

Elaina replied, 'That's perfectly fine, son.'

'Yeah, that's understandable. We'll stand in for you,' Calvin told his son while giving him a pat on the back. 'Thank you', replied Corey." (pg. 195)

It is important to hear the heart of a person, whether it be as a parent, friend, co-worker, teacher, etc. Elaina and Calvin had compassion for their son because they knew exactly what he had been through and were not going to force him to attend the sentencing of Darren. They heard his heart, and I'm sure he was glad that they did. We should not force someone to do something they are uncomfortable with just because we are comfortable with it. God is a compassionate God, which is a trait we all should have. There are so many people in the world who are suffering or hurting on the inside and sometimes just needs a listening ear and some compassion. A little compassion goes a long way and may even open the door for you to pray for them.

The word of God says in…

Colossians 3:12

"Put on therefore, as the elect of God, holy and beloved, bowels of mercies, kindness, humbleness of mind, meekness, longsuffering;"

2 Corinthians 1:3-4

"Blessed be God, even the Father of our Lord Jesus Christ, the Father of mercies, and the God of all comfort; Who comforteth us in all our tribulation, that we may be able to comfort them which are in any trouble, by the comfort wherewith we ourselves are comforted of God."

Galatians 6:2

"Bear ye one another's burdens, and so fulfil the law of Christ."

Food for thought:

Over time, I've had to learn how to listen more and talk less. I also used to shy away from praying for people out in public, but had to repent for all of that. I started thinking… what if my listening and/or prayer puts a smile on a person's face or even saves a life? That's right… I had to work on being more compassionate than I was. I'm still working on it; however, I'm much better. So, I want to encourage you to take a moment to listen to and see if you can hear that person's heart who may be trying to tell you they are hurting. And should the door open for prayer, pray for them on the spot because your prayer just may be the prayer they need to put a smile on their face or save their life.

Here are some questions for you to consider:

1. Have you ever had the opportunity to pray for someone that really needed it and you did not do it because you were in public and/or afraid? *(Yes or No)* Be honest…

2. If yes, briefly explain what happened.

3. Do you now feel you are at a place in your faith where you would be able to pray for them or anyone if need be, out in public if the opportunity arises? *(Yes or No)* If your answer is no, you may want to join a ministry that will give you plenty of practice doing so.

Chapter 36

"Leave The Vengeance To God"

"Calvin could sense that Elaina was getting upset, so he grabbed her hand. She looked over at Darren whose head was still down. 'I want you to know, Darren, I forgive you for what you did. And I pray God deals with you while you're behind bars. I'm not gonna say what sentence you deserve. It's God's wrath you have to worry about,' said Elaina, and she looked back up at the judge. 'Thank you, your Honor.' Elaina continued to hold on to Calvin's hand as they walked back to their seats." (pg. 200-201)

This could not have been easy for Elaina; however, she humbled herself and forgave Darren. Not only did she take a blow with Calvin's situation, but with Corey's situation as well which I'm sure was worse. Although she was angry as all get out, she is leaving the wrath and vengeance to God. It takes extreme faith to do what Elaina did. People get so bent out of shape in seeking revenge with those who have hurt them, without realizing that God's wrath and punishment is worse than anything we can ever dish out.

The word of God says in…

Romans 12:19

"Dearly beloved, avenge not yourselves, but rather give place unto wrath: for it is written, Vengeance is mine; I will repay, saith the Lord."

Romans 13:4

"For he is the minister of God to thee for good. But if thou do that which is evil, be afraid; for he beareth not the sword in vain: for he is the minister of God, a revenger to execute wrath upon him that doeth evil."

Ezekiel 25:17

"And I will execute great vengeance upon them with furious rebukes; and they shall know that I am the LORD, when I shall lay my vengeance upon them."

Food for thought:

I remember getting even with this girl by fighting her when I was in elementary school. The only way I would fight is if the other person started it. Well, this girl started it, and I remember giving her a beat down that she would never forget. I felt good about it at that moment, but looking back, I realized that was bad. That was the first and last time I got into a fight. And ever since then, when someone hurt or offended me, God has always taken care of it. I stopped having bitterness and staying angry with people who offended or hurt me, especially as I got older because I knew God would execute his wrath and vengeance on my behalf. Now, I easily forgive, release them, and turn them over to God. So, I say to you, when someone offends or hurt you, let God handle it the way He wants to and in His own time.

Here are some questions for you to consider:

1. Have you ever tried to get even with someone who offended or hurt you? *(Yes or No)* Be honest…

2. If so, what did you do?

3. After you retaliated, how did you feel?

4. How do you feel about it now?

Chapter 37

"They Still Need Your Prayers"

"'You know what we need to do now?' asked Elaina.

David answered, 'Forget we ever knew him, right?'

Elaina and Calvin chuckled. 'Boy, no,' Elaina replied. 'We need to pray for him: for protection and that he comes to know God while he's in there. Who knows… he may be able to get out of there early if he has good behavior.'" (pg. 204-205)

Here, Elaina continues to be the example of Christ that her family needs to see. Elaina still feels sorry for Darren, which is understandable since she's known him since they were young and is considered family. Praying for and continuing to love those that hurt or offended you, is just as important as forgiving them. Yeah, I know… this is pushing it, right? Well, this is actually a directive from God. Again, they are entitled to a clean slate just as you are.

The word of God says in…

Matthew 5:44

"But I say unto you, Love your enemies, bless them that curse you, do good to them that hate you, and pray for them which despitefully use you and persecute you;"

1 Peter 3:9

"Not rendering evil for evil, or railing for railing: but contrariwise blessing; knowing that ye are thereunto called, that ye should inherit a blessing."

Proverbs 24:17-18

"Rejoice not when thine enemy falleth, and let not thine heart be glad when he stumbleth: Lest the LORD see it, and it displease him, and he turn away is wrath from him."

Food for thought:

Prayer really does change things… and people. You saw this with Elaina some chapters back. If you find it hard to do this for those that hurt or offended you, start out with just praying for their heart to be convicted for what they did to you. Then hopefully, as you draw closer to God and He repairs your wounds, it will become easier for you to pray for them to where you're even comfortable with praying a blessing over them.

Here are some questions for you to consider:

1. Do you find it <u>easy</u> or <u>hard</u> to pray for those who hurt or offend you?

2. Briefly explain the reason for your answer to #1.

3. And lastly, here is a challenge for you: For the next 21 days, *pray* a blessing for all of those who have hurt or offended you. During this challenge, you may even find yourself being blessed. If so, please share with me at <u>changeofheartmovie@gmail.com</u>.

Chapter 38

"Let's Go Fishing"

"Corey said, 'Granddad, thanks for taking us fishing,'

'You're welcome, Corey.'" (pg. 212)

"'Dad, you were right. This did take my mind off of... you know,' said Corey.

'Good. I'm sure we'll do it again soon.' Calvin replied, as he tapped Corey on the arm with his elbow. He looked at David. 'Right, David?'

'Well, I don't think this fishing thing is for me. I'll just stick to football and just stay home next time.'" (pg. 213)

Poor David... fishing just did not work out for him... at least not on this trip, but it seemed to be great therapy for Corey. And I must agree with Corey. Fishing can be very relaxing and take your mind off of things. You either love it or hate it. I happen to love fishing! With that being said...

It's game time! Let's see how much you know about fishing! This game is called "How Well Do You Know Fishing Slang?"! This can be played individually or as a group. If playing as a group, make it even more exciting by giving a prize to the person who has the highest score.

Here are the instructions:

1. Open up a browser on one of your devices and type in, How Well Do You Know Fishing Slang? This game is by How Stuff Works. Click on it.?

2. You will see an orange button that says "Read More" which you may click on to learn more about this challenge, or you can go ahead and start the challenge. You may need to use the Hint button a few times on this one... or who knows, you may not. Either way...

Have fun fishing for the answers!

Chapter 39

"Pick Your Bone Carefully"

"'You know, I've been thinking… I believe it's time for me to pay someone a visit,' Calvin said as he cut a piece of his sausage on his plate and placed it in his mouth.

She asked, 'Who?'

'Darren.'

'Really?'

'Yeah. I think it's time for me to ask him some questions I've been wondering about. I couldn't do it six months ago, Laina. I would've killed him if I had the chance.' Calvin said, as he stuffed his mouth with eggs." (pg. 215)

After several months, Calvin is ready to confront Darren. If you have a bone to pick with someone who has wronged you in some way, make sure you do it in love or cordially. If you're not ready to do that, then hold off until you are. Calvin said if he would have gone to see Darren any earlier, he would have killed him. I absolutely believe that would have taken place, especially before he rededicated his life to God. In any case, God gives us permission to address our offenses. Again, as discussed in a previous chapter, doing so prevents deep rooted anger and bitterness. This falls in line with reconciliation.

The word of God says this…

Matthew 18:15

"Moreover if thy brother shall trespass against thee, go and tell him his fault between thee and him alone: if he shall hear thee, thou hast gained thy brother."

Galatians 6:1

"Brethren, if a man be overtaken in a fault, ye which are spiritual, restore such a one in the spirit of meekness; considering thyself, lest thou also be tempted."

Proverbs 29:11

"A fool uttereth all his mind: but a wise man keepeth it in till afterwards."

Food for thought:

Earlier in life, when someone offended me, I used to not say anything and hold my anger in which produced resentment against that person. Doing so, did not accomplish anything. As I've come to know God more, now when someone offends me, I ask Him how He wants me to handle it. Sometimes He will tell me not to say anything, and in those situations, it works itself out. And in other times, He will give me exactly what to say, how and when to say it. When that is the case, the person has always apologized and thanked me for bringing it to their attention that they offended me. When you pick your bone God's way, who knows, it may lead to a correction of how that person says or do things to someone. Well, God knows… He knows everything. So, pick your bone carefully.

Here are some questions for you to consider:

1. When someone offends you, do you pick a bone with that person *(or say anything to them)*? *(Yes or No)*

2. Depending on how you answered #1, what is typically the outcome?

3. Do you seek God when you need to pick a bone with someone? *(Yes or No)* Be Honest…

4. And lastly, what is the typical outcome when someone picks a bone with you?

Chapter 40

"Hit Reverse On The Generational Curse"

"Tears rolled down Darren's face. 'I know. I'm sorry, man. I really am,' he told him as he wiped his face. 'C.J., I never told anyone this… but when I was ten, I had an uncle on my dad's side who… touched and did stuff to me,' explained Darren.

'So, let me get this… to fix what happened to you, you repeat what he did by doing that to other kids? There's something wrong with that, man.'" (pg. 224)

Do you remember how I said in Chapter 26 that history can be repeating itself, unfortunately, with Darren, and that we would discuss this more in detail at a later time? It's that time. It is unfortunate that *in most cases*, an offender or abuser has been through what they have done or are doing to others, at some point in time in their lives. This is considered a **generational curse** which Satan uses to destroy families. That is why once a generational curse is recognized in one's family, BEHEAD it quickly!

Let's see what the word of God says about generational curses…

Ezekiel 18:20

"The soul that sinneth, it shall die. The son shall not bear the iniquity of the father, neither shall the father bear the iniquity of the son: the righteousness of the righteous shall be upon him, and the wickedness of the wicked shall be upon him."

Exodus 34:7

"Keeping mercy for thousands, forgiving iniquity and transgression and sin, and that will by no means clear the guilty; visiting the iniquity of the fathers upon the children, and upon the children's children, unto the third and to the fourth generation."

Deuteronomy 30:19

"I call heaven and earth to record this day against you, that I have set before you life and death, blessing and cursing: therefore choose life, that both thou and thy seed may live:"

Food for thought:

The way to behead generational curses is by constantly confessing the blessings of the Lord over your family. Just as there are Bible verses about generational curses, there are also Bible verses about generational blessings, starting off with the Book of Genesis. So, begin reversing those generational curses by praying generational blessings over your family.

Here are some questions for you to consider:

1. Do you believe your family *(this may include outside of your immediate family)* has generational curses? *(Yes or No)*

2. If so, how do you know? Briefly explain.

3. Name 2 examples of a generational curse.

Chapter 41

"How Will They Know?"

"'He really didn't have an explanation for why he messed with those boys and Corey, but he dropped a bombshell on me.'

'Dropped a bombshell? What was it?' asked Elaina.

'He said when he was ten, he had an uncle who did the same stuff to him.' Her mouth dropped open. Calvin said, 'I know. I couldn't believe it either. When he told me that, I kind of felt sorry for him. Then I brought up the point that he didn't fix the problem by repeating it.'" (pg. 227)

"'Right!' Elaina exclaimed. 'Wow.' She was still stunned by that news.

'Yeah,' Calvin said, as he nodded. 'He actually started crying when I mentioned Corey's name.'

'I almost feel that I should keep visiting him.'

'Maybe you should. You never know; that can help him, too. And take the Bible with you while you at it so you can share some Word with him.'

'I don't know how to do that. I'm just now really learning it myself,' he explained. 'I'll take him a Bible, and he can read it for himself,' Calvin said." (pg. 228)

What a transformation God is doing through Calvin these days! He's talking about visiting Darren more and even taking him a Bible. Over several months back when he was bitter with his dad, he could care less about a Bible. Although Elaina and Calvin are highly disappointed with Darren, they still have compassion for him especially after learning about what happened to him as a child and desires for him to be helped. Regardless of what he did, he is still a child of God. This is what it's all about! When God transforms your life, He desires for you to help others do the same whether you are a babe in Christ or thirty years in. How will the lost and hurting know how they can become free if we, who have been saved and delivered, do not tell them.

The word of God says in…

Hebrews 13:16

"But to do good and to communicate forget not: for with such sacrifices God is well pleased."

1 John 3:17

"But whoso hath this world's good, and seeth his brother have need, and shutteth up his bowels of compassion from him, how dwelleth the love of God in him?"

Proverbs 11:25

"The liberal soul shall be made fat: and he that watereth shall be watered also himself."

Food for thought:

The only way people will truly change from the wicked ways of this world is if they have an encounter with Jesus Christ. The only way that will happen is if people see Jesus Christ in you. Sharing God's word is a part of it; however, it all boils down to sharing what the Lord has done for you and living your life as an example of Him for others to see. And just like we need God, God needs us to be that extension of Christ to help the hurting and the lost in this world.

Here are some questions for you to consider:

1. Briefly share your testimony of how you came to know Jesus for yourself.

2. If you know God, but haven't received His son as your Lord and Savior, now is the time to do so if you want to make sure Heaven will be your eternal home. For Jesus said, "I am the way, the truth, and the life: no man cometh unto the Father, but by me. *(John 14:6)*" Have your group leader pray with you or some-one you know that has the capabilities of leading you to Christ.

Chapter 42

"Let Me Remind You"

"'You remember when I told you and your brother that, 'Jesus would never leave or forsake you, no matter how hard it got in your life'?'

'Yes, sir.'

'Well, it's true, Corey. It was no surprise to God what happened to you.'

'Then why did He allow it to happen?'

'Well Corey, the devil causes bad things to happen to people, not God. And it's usually because of the choices we humans make. In your case, it was nothing you did. So, don't blame yourself,' he told Corey." (pg. 232)

Corey desperately needed this talk with Pastor Gillesby. It is key for you to know that although bad things happen by no surprise to God, He is not the blame. I mentioned this in a previous chapter. God does not make a person do anything. He gives us free will to make our own decisions, good or bad. However, He promises to always be there for us. That is why when Satan throws a wrench in our lives for which **God has already mapped out for us**, He has to come in and clean up the damage done by Satan. Going through something like Corey is going through can feel like a long and lonely walk; however, know you are not alone. God reminds us of this constantly in His word.

The word of God says in…

Deuteronomy 31:8

"And the Lord, he it is that doth go before thee; he will be thee, he will not fail thee, neither forsake thee: fear not, neither be dismayed."

Joshua 1:9

"Have not I commanded thee? Be strong and of a good courage; be not afraid, neither be thou dismayed: for the LORD thy God is with thee withersoever thou goest."

Isaiah 41:10-13

"Fear thou not; for I am with thee: be not dismayed; for I am thy God: I will strengthen thee; yea, I will help thee; yea, I will uphold thee with the right hand of my righteousness. Behold, all they that were incensed against thee shall be ashamed and confounded: they shall be as nothing; and they that strive with thee shall perish. Thou shalt seek them, and shalt not find them, even them that contended with thee: they that war against thee shall be as nothing, and as a thing of nought. For I the LORD thy God will hold thy right hand, saying unto thee, Fear not; I will help thee."

Food for thought:

That was just a few verses in the Bible about not being forsaken by God. There is a plethora of verses to make sure you never forget that you are not alone and not to fear. God is making sure you get this. So, *whatever* you're going through, you do not have to go through it alone. God already has people in place to help you with your situation or circumstance, but you must surrender your will for His and just say "yes" like Corey did... and like I did. I didn't even know I was still hurting until I opened my heart up to God.

Here are some questions for you to consider:

1. In this chapter of the novel on page 233, Pastor Gillesby told Corey, God will take a bad situation and turn it into a good one. Corey took a moment and realized that there were a few good things that happened while dealing with his crisis. What were they?

2. Was there ever a time in your life where you felt alone and scared while enduring a tough situation, and God sent someone to be there for you until you got through it? *(Yes or No)*

3. If so, who was that person *(mom/dad, sibling, teacher, coach, pastor, guardian angel, etc.)* for you?

Never ever forget... you are not alone!

Chapter 43

"Speak Up"

"'Yeah, I went and saw Darren a few days ago at the prison.'

'You did? What for?'

'Because I needed answers for myself.'

'Oh… okay,' Corey replied." (pg. 237)

"'I wanted to know why he did those things to you and those other boys.'

'What did he say?'

'He couldn't give me an answer. He did tell me though… the same thing happened to him when he was ten.'

'It did?'

'That's what he said. Doesn't make an excuse for him to do that to other boys.'

'No, it doesn't,' replied Corey, as he dropped his eyes off of his dad and on to the table, remembering that vivid day Darren touched him. 'I believe if he would've told someone about it back then, who knows… he probably wouldn't be in the situation he's in now.' Corey looked back up at his dad. 'Well Dad, I wasn't going to say anything either, to you or mom. I really didn't want to say anything to David, but I figured he wouldn't say anything.' Corey explained. 'Guess I should've reevaluated that.'

'No, I'm glad you said something to somebody. And I'm glad David had sense enough to let your mom know,' Calvin stated." (pg. 238)

Corey doesn't realize speaking up about what Darren did to him was the best thing he could have ever done. Another one of my goals with this story is to bring about child sexual abuse awareness and to encourage kids to "SPEAK UP." And although I'm specifically addressing child sexual abuse, ANY sexual (this includes incest) or physical abuse to anyone should be reported. Staying silent will bring about more harm than speaking up. I'm sure there are a lot of these incidents that have been swept under a rug in order to keep peace or fear of no one believing the incident(s) really happened. For me as a young girl, it was fear of no one believing me and being in trouble for it. Now, I know better and want to try and help as many people as I can. If you're not a victim of abuse, however, know someone in any of these situations, "SPEAK UP." This falls in line with the saying, "if you see something, say something." Our bodies are not our own… they belong to God, and should be treated as such, with respect and dignity.

The word of God says in…

Ephesians 5:11-13

"And have no fellowship with the unfruitful works of darkness, but rather reprove them. For it is a shame even to speak of those things which are done of them in secret. But all things that are reproved are made manifest by the light: for whatso ever doth make manifest is light."

1 Corinthians 6:19-20

"What? know ye not that your body is the temple of the Holy Ghost which is in you, which ye have of God, and ye are not your own? For ye are bought with a price: therefore glorify God in your body, and in your spirit, which are God's."

Food for thought:

When these immoral acts happened to me as a little girl, I had no clue that it was wrong. And I do not remember if I portrayed any behavior in front of my parents to indicate that I was molested. I do remember, however, running away at the age of twelve because I felt I wasn't loved. This could have very well been a product of what happened to me as a little girl… I don't know. I say all this to encourage parents to pay attention to your kids' behavior if it seems odd. Action speaks louder than words. And if you are an adult going through any kind of abuse, please don't stay silent. We are meant to live victoriously, not victimized.

Here are some questions for you to consider:

1. In Chapter 25, I indicated two national abuse hotlines that anyone can call should they need to. What are they?

Remember, "you are a chosen generation, a royal priesthood, an holy nation, a peculiar people; that you should shew forth the praises of him who hath called you out of darkness into his marvellous light:" *(1 Peter 2:9)* And you were made to live victoriously, not victimized.

Chapter 44

"Get Out Of Your Comfort Zone"

"'Hey C.J., I wasn't expecting another visit from you,' Darren said as he sat down across from Calvin.

'Yeah. I wasn't expecting another visit from me either, but it wasn't up to me. And this time I figured it would be okay not to have a glass wall in between us.' Darren chuckled a bit and said, 'Laina told you to come?'

'No. I think the good man upstairs wanted me to do this... definitely not something I would do on my own.' Calvin said. 'Laina did suggest I bring this to you though.' He pushed the Bible over to him.

Darren did a quick flip through, looking at it as if he was familiar with it at one time. 'Preciate it.'"
(pg. 242)

You know God is at work when you begin to do things you would not typically do on your own. Calvin told Darren he was not expecting to visit him again and that it was the man upstairs that wanted him to come. MOST of the time, when God has a specific task for you to do, it will be out of your comfort zone. However, as I stated in the Chapter 42, God said not to fear because He's with you. How is He with us? I'm so glad you asked... By the tangible presence of His son, Jesus, along with the help of the Holy Spirit. With their help, you can carry out ANY task He gives you, whether it's small, big, have the necessary education or not. He just needs you to say, "Yes!"

The word of God says in...

Matthew 19:26

"But Jesus beheld them, and said unto them, With men this is impossible, but with God all things are possible."

Mark 9:23

"Jesus said unto him, If thou canst believe, all things are possible to him that believeth."

Ephesians 3:20

"Now unto him that is able to do exceeding abundantly above all that we ask or think, according to the power that worketh in us,"

Food for thought:

I can attest that when God gives you an assignment, He will give you the necessary tools you need to accomplish the task at hand. I never thought I would be able to write a book, study guide, and movie, all without a degree. At first, I felt overwhelmed and fearful to move forward with all of these until I totally surrendered to Him and told Him "Yes, I'll do it IF He showed me how and what to do." And He has done just that with all three tasks. So, everything you see and hear comes straight from God. And I am just a vessel that has yielded my gifts and talents to Him, for which He gave to me in the first place. I got out of my comfort zone.

Here are some questions for you to consider:

1. What has been, thus far, your *biggest* task given to you by God to do?

2. Have you completed it OR in the process of completing it? *(Yes or No)*

3. If yes, what was the outcome?

4. If no, what is holding you back or what are you waiting for?

Chapter 45

"An Encounter Worth Remembering"

"Calvin shouted, 'The man of the hour is here!'

'Hey everybody!' Tony shouted, as the guys rushed to meet him. Calvin allowed everyone to greet Tony first before he approached him. After everyone had greeted and congratulated him, he walked up to him. He hadn't seen him in person since the altercation in Dallas. 'What's up, man?' Calvin said as he and Tony embraced. 'It sure is nice not to be greeted with a fist this time.'

Tony laughed and said, 'Whatever, man. Good to see you.' He looked around. 'C.J. man, this is nice.'" (pg. 250)

"'All for you, my man… all for you. Well, let's get some food and see what these other guys been up to. I'm still waiting for Philip to show. You know how that is.'

'Yeah. He'll get here when it's time to go home.'" (pg. 251)

It's good to see that Calvin and T.B.'s encounter this time is for a celebration. T.B.'s bachelor party for his upcoming wedding! And their college buddies came to help T.B. celebrate. These guys knew a lot about each other while attending college together; however, it's been years since they've seen each other, which means some things could have changed over time with each of them. You may be doing this study with a group of people you have known for a long time or not. By this time, you should have learned some things about the people in your group. See just how much you have learned about them by playing the last game in this study guide. *(Unfortunately, this game can only be played with a group.)*

This game is called "Likes and Dislikes."

Here are the instructions:

- You will need some index cards and pens to play.

- Ask everyone to write down 5 of their likes and 5 of their dislikes on index cards.

- Have one person collect them all, mix them up and read the cards one at a time. *(This person will need to be designated as the moderator of the game who will just collect the cards and read them.)*

- Everyone else will need to guess whose likes and dislikes belong to whom. *(Again, this is just for fun; no score needs to be taken.)*

Have fun learning more about your group!

Chapter 46

"Forsake Not Your Family"
(pg. 256-262)

For this chapter, I don't have a specific excerpt from the novel to talk about; however, I want to shine a light on "family". So, take this as my personal comments and "food for thought" all combined. I believe there are a lot of families out there like the Hardy family who can relate to them. As you can see by now, they have been on a roller coaster ride for the past several months dealing with all kinds of situations, some at the same time; however, through it all, they defeated and continue to defeat Satan's schemes. That is because the pillar of the family, Elaina, never gave up on praying. This family also has a strong covering who covers them in prayer and counsel when needed, such as Pastor Gillesby and Mother Newsome.

It's kind of cliché', but so true… a family that prays together, stays together. We as believers are quick to minister to or pray for people outside of our families, but tend to sometimes neglect those right in our household and/or family members outside of our household. And even sometimes give up on praying for certain family members when we don't see change in them. I've been guilty of not necessarily giving up on praying for them, however, forgetting to pray for them. I can say today I've gotten much better at it.

The word of God says in…

1 Timothy 5:8

"But if any provide not for his own, and specially for those of his own house, he hath denied the faith, and is worse than an infidel."

Proverbs 11:29

"He that troubleth his own house shall inherit the wind: and the fool shall be servant to the wise of heart."

Proverbs 15:27

"He that is greedy of gain troubleth his own house; but he that hateth gifts shall live."

Joshua 24:15

"And if it seem evil unto you to serve the LORD, choose you this day whom ye will serve; whether the gods which your fathers served that were on the other side of the flood, or the gods of the Amorites, in whose land ye dwell: but as for me and my house we, will serve the LORD."

Here are some questions for you to consider:

1. Who do you consider the pillar *(source of strength or rock)* of your household or immediate family?

2. Briefly explain the reason for your answer to #1.

3. List the names of family members you know are heading down the wrong path or not saved.

4. Now all you have to do is pray for them often, and when the opportunity arises, share the word of God with them.

Chapter 47

"Who Is Left To Train Them?"

"Mother Newsome nodded and replied, 'That's definitely God,' while she continued to chow down on her food and watch a young African-American woman in her mid-twenties order her food at the counter. Elaina's back was facing the young woman; however, she could tell that something had Mother Newsome's attention. The young woman had on a pair of denim low waist high cut shorts, revealing a portion of her bottom and a really low cut top. 'Would you look at that?' asked Mother Newsome. Elaina turned around to see what she was talking about. She said, 'I just don't know about some of these women. They just don't leave any of their private goods covered up these days.'" (pg. 264-265)

"Mother Newsome finally ceased staring the young woman down and focused her attention back on Elaina. She said, 'I'm sorry, baby. It's just that when I see women dressed like that, showing everything… it disturbs me.'

'I agree,' Elaina replied while nodding. 'That's why I'm careful of how I dress in front of Trina. And make sure she dresses modestly, too.'" (pg. 265)

Are there still any Mother Newsome's out there in the world? If you know of any, cherish and respect them. I believe the world is short on these mothers. They are mothers that would lay the truth on you, regardless of who you belonged to and no matter if you were female or male. And it really does take a village to raise children these days; however, you almost need a permit to say anything to them. What Mother Newsome was talking about regarding the young woman was absolutely correct. There are so many women these days wearing more of their bodies than clothing, revealing more than what needs to be revealed. Elaina said she's careful how she dresses in front of Trina and makes sure Trina dresses modestly too. What parents fail to realize is that children are on loan to them from God. And He's watching how we raise and treat His children. Children mimic what they see, hear, and grow up around. If they see you being disrespectful or using profanity like it's your native language, then they will do the same outside of the home, inside of the home, and even towards you. If they see you dressing inappropriately, then they will think it's okay to do the same.

The word of God says in…

Proverbs 22:6

"Train up a child in the way he should go: and when he is old, he will not depart from it."

Isaiah 54:13

"And all thy children shall be taught of the LORD; and great shall be the peace of thy children."

Ephesians 6:1-4

"Children, obey your parents in the Lord: for this is right. Honour thy father and mother; (which is the first commandment with promise;) That it may be well with thee, and thou mayest live long on the earth. And, ye fathers, provoke not your children to wrath: but bring them up in the nurture and admonition of the Lord."

Food for thought:

Although I'm thankful for my parents, I'm tremendously grateful for my grandparents, maternal and fraternal. They all were praying grandparents, and I believe I would not be who I am today had it not been for their prayers. It is imperative that children have Godly pillars in their lives to nurture and ensure they grow up as Godly pillars themselves.

Here are some questions for you to consider:

1. Did you have, or do you have a Mother Newsome type figure in your life *(parent, grandparent, etc.)*? *(Yes or No)*

2. If so, how has this person impacted your life?

3. There is an old saying "Each one, teach one". In what ways are you helping the next generation coming up after you? *(It does not matter what age you are. If you are old enough to do this study guide, you are old enough to make a difference in the lives of the next generation.)*

Remember… every child in the village eventually becomes one of the village elders.

Chapter 48

"Some People Just Know"

"Calvin chuckled a little. 'I have to tell you something,' he said, as he sat down with her. Elaina asked, 'What? Is it bad?'

'No not at all. A co-worker of mine asked me to pray for him.'

'Really?' asked Elaina while smiling from ear to ear.

'Yeah. When he came to my office asking me that, I had to look behind me to make sure he wasn't talking to somebody else. And then I still had to ask, 'You want me to pray for you?' He said, 'Yeah, I do.' He's a white guy who's an architectural draftsman. He's the one that used to live in Dallas.'

'Well, where did you pray for him?'

'Right there in my office. I shut the blinds and closed the door. And said to myself, 'Okay, God… you gone give me what to say, right?' and He did just that.'

'Wow… I'm speechless,' replied Elaina. 'He just wanted you to pray for him or was it for something specific?'

'He just found out he has cancer.'" (pg. 270)

"'I didn't tell him I was a Christian. So, I don't know why he asked me.'

'You don't have to tell people you're a Christian. Some people can just sense it,' Elaina explained. 'I bet you had no idea God would use you like this.'" (pg. 271)

Remember, I told you in Chapter 22, you are being watched by somebody. Calvin's co-worker didn't know he would end up with cancer, and neither he nor Calvin knew that Calvin would be the one to pray for him at that moment, on that day; however, God did. Again, God brings people into our lives for a reason. Nothing happens by coincidence. Calvin's transformation has his light shining bright enough where this man sees it and draws him to Calvin for prayer. That is how it should be. We should not have to tell people we are believers of Christ. It should portray in everything we do and/or say.

The word of God says in…

Matthew 5:14-16

"Ye are the light of the world. A city that is set on an hill cannot be hid. Neither do men light a candle, and put it under a bushel, but on a candlestick; and it giveth light unto all that are in the house. Let your light so shine before men, that they may see your good works, and glorify your Father which is in heaven."

Ephesians 5:8

"For ye were sometimes darkness, but now are ye light in the Lord: walk as children of light:"

2 Corinthians 5:20

"Now then we are ambassadors for Christ, as though God did beseech you by us: we pray you in Christ's stead, be ye reconciled to God."

Food for thought:

What happened to Calvin, happened to me several years ago when I worked in corporate. However, my experience was a little different. During a normal workday, I received an email which was part of a group email sent out asking to meet and pray for a co-worker whose cancer had returned. So, about six or so people, which included me and this particular co-worker, retreated to a meeting room that wasn't being used. And the person who sent out the email kind of explained that this co-worker was going back in to be tested and wanted the group to pray for him. Now, there were a few people in this group that I didn't know was even a Christian until that moment. And then to my surprise, I was asked to pray for this man. I did not mind praying back then, however, was wondering why they chose me to pray. Nevertheless, I told the group that I would be praying in the name of Jesus *(to give warning to those that may not believe in Him)*, then laid hands on this man. I don't remember what I prayed, but I know I declared that he was healed in Jesus name. Some weeks later, I found out that he went back in for testing and the cancer was gone! I came to realize that this was all set up by God himself.

Here are some questions for you to consider:

1. Have you ever had an experience like me or Calvin, outside of church? (Yes or No)

2. If so, briefly explain.

If no, then you never know when you may be next. Just be ready to be used by God at any moment and at any time. Again, "some people just know" you have exactly what they need, and that is a touch from God himself.

Notes

_____

_____

_____

_____

_____

_____

_____

_____

_____

_____

_____

_____

_____

_____

_____

_____

Notes

_____

_____

_____

_____

_____

_____

_____

_____

_____

_____

_____

_____

_____

_____

_____

_____

Made in the USA
Columbia, SC
19 March 2021